T0328415

Beyond Appearances

Beyond Appearances

Reflections on Principles and Practice

DAVID HAROLD BARRY, SJ

Published by Weaver Press, Box A1922, Avondale, Harare.
2018
<www.weaverpresszimbabwe.com>

Typeset by Weaver Press
Cover Design Weaver Press
Printed by Directory Publishers, Bulawayo

Cover photographs: Front cover Weaver Press
Back cover courtesy of Maria Imbrova

The author and publisher would like to express their
gratitude to Trōcaire, Zimbabwe for their contribution towards
the printing costs.

ISBN: 918-1-77922-329-5 (p/b)
ISBN: 918-1-77922-340-1 (epub)

DAVID HAROLD BARRY, SJ is a Jesuit priest from Ireland who spent 25 years with Silveira House, a Leadership Training and Development Centre in Zimbabwe. His first fourteen years in the country were in pre-Independence Rhodesia, when fear wrestled with idealism, and the subsequent 36 years, in independent Zimbabwe when idealism was crushed by self-interest.

Beyond his work in administration and training he discovered an interest in observing and reflecting on people with a culture that differed from his own. He was invited to write a weekly column, the fruit of these reflections, in *The Zimbabwean*, a weekly paper which flourished for ten years of this century before succumbing to financial constraints.

Though a priest with a calling to proclaim the good news of Jesus, he is drawn to look at the lives of people first and only then to discern, within ordinary events, the seeds of what Jesus was struggling to portray to an often bewildered audience. In this endeavour Harold Barry also edited two books: *They Stayed On* which tells the story of the seven Jesuits who were killed in the liberation war; and *Zimbabwe, the Past is the Future*, essays which examine how past policies and experiences will inevitably affect the trajectory of a country.

CONTENTS

PART TWO: DISCOVERING OUR IMAGINATION

PART THREE: HOPE IN SOLIDARITY

PART FOUR: THE INSPIRATION OF PEOPLE

Foreword

'Only connect the prose and the passion, and both will be
exalted, and human love will be seen at its highest. Live in
fragments no longer.'

E.M. Forster, *Howards End,*

F orster's advice excites us to find ways of linking our words
to our experience. Are we inclined to think words can stand
on their own like dollar notes with a face value no matter who
is handling them? Do we sometimes explain the scriptures
without reference to our hearers? The only time Jesus gave a full
course on scripture, on the way to Emmaus, he started with his
listeners' experience.

Effective communication has to be a dialogue. I love those words
of Papa Francis; '[We] have the wonderful but difficult task of joining
loving hearts: the hearts of the Lord and of his people' (*The Joy of the
Gospel* #143). To teach, to preach or to write is to listen, and to be
ready to be changed by what we hear.

Eleven years ago I was asked by Wilf and Trish Mbanga to write
a column for their new paper, *The Zimbabwean*. They left me free to
write what I wanted. I extended that freedom by writing under a
pseudonym, *Ngomakurira* (drum sounds), but it didn't help. When
eventually my inner censor slipped for a moment, I wrote words
that were seen as a threat and there were consequences. But what
I perceived as freedom at least nudged me to write as I wanted and
slowly I moved out of my head. My heart was edging its way in.

'The heart has its reasons,' said Pascal, 'which reason does not
know.' I was drawn to perch on experience. What did I feel when I

saw or heard or read something. Often I was moved by good news as well as bad. As I tried to absorb and dwell on it a word of Jesus would come to me, illuminating the experience. It felt like poetry. Each week, for more than ten years, I looked forward to my tryst with words.

It was normal to have no idea what I would write. But always something would emerge. In time I began to browse the Sunday scripture – not for ideas – but for buried roots. The gospel is not 'out there' for us to harness and tame. It is within all things waiting to emerge, like sculpture from rough stone.

Sometimes you will find that I have quoted the words of a personality that I had recently heard speak on the radio, or comment in a pamphlet or article. We have done our best to reference these quotations, so topical at the time, but have not always been able to find the exact reference.

Anyway, every week, 500 words would appear. I felt they were worth keeping, binding each hundred articles and brazenly lodging them in our Jesuit archives with the view that others might look at them a century from now.

Alas, that hundred years is up. Janice McLaughlin, Arkmore Kori and Nora Brodrick kindly waded through some of the more than five hundred *ngomas* and made the selection you hold in your hands. Ruth Bakare, wife of the former bishop of Manicaland, discerns in them 'a unique way of contextualising the Bible'. I found this confirmation of what I was trying to do: not starting with the scriptures and 'applying' them to experience. Rather it was the other way round: starting with experience and seeing how the gospel makes it catch fire. So I would like to thank the six people mentioned above and the others who have encouraged me to continue. I would be happy if these words give a little alleluia to those of Hopkins: 'Christ plays in ten thousand places ... Lovely in limbs, and lovely in eyes not his.'

David Harold-Barry, Lusaka, 2016

PART 1

ABANDONED, YET STRUGGLING

1

STRUGGLING IN SMALL WAYS

Zimbabwe suffers from a broken self-image. The halftime scoreboard doesn't look good.

We bounced into action in 1980 full of enthusiasm and ideas but almost from that moment things started to go wrong. The woes of the past 25 years need no listing here. But perhaps we have not looked sufficiently at how they arose. Joshua Nkomo wrote in the 1980s, 'the hardest lesson of my life came to me late. It is that a nation can win freedom without its people becoming free.' Many nations have won their freedom through violence. But violence sows a seed that must at some stage be exorcised or else it will eat into the fabric of society. In 1931, Gandhi said, 'I personally would wait, if need be for ages, rather than seek to attain the freedom of my country through bloody means.' Many admired Gandhi, including Nkomo. Few leaders, including our own, had the stature to say such a thing. Violence is, in a sense, easier but it leaves a terrible heritage.

And we are the heirs now. We are reaping the whirlwind.

Violence sits enthroned in our country and all significant decisions need her backing. She will not retire easily. The call to each one of us is to strive mightily against her. It calls for a revolution of the heart, not in some vague pious sermon, but in the hard reality of your day and mine. We have to confront every injustice starting with the smallest. I was struck, in Mandela's autobiography, by his insistence on wearing long trousers on Robben Island. He struggled for that. Then he struggled for something else; then something else. Finally South Africa was free.

Years ago, in the 1970s in Mabvuku, the youth started a campaign called Courtesy is Contagious. They monitored people getting on buses and made sure the elderly or women with babies got on first. Little things. But little things become big things. (The Rhodesians of the time knew this and they banned the campaign).

No one questions our need for change in our country today, except the minority who fatten themselves on the status quo. But equally we seem paralysed from working for that change by the threat of violence. Somewhere, somehow, we have to fight our own fear. Until we do that we will remain in thrall.

2 March, 2005

2

FIDDLING WHILE ROME BURNS

Hungry, thirsty, a stranger, naked, sick or in prison: these are the dire conditions listed in Matthew, chapter 25, which afflict people of every age and place and cry out for attention.

The British *Spectator* devoted a recent article to ways of cooking and serving hake, a fish the Spanish scoop from the seas around Europe so that stocks are now 'outside safe biological limits according to the Marine Conservation Society. The British supermarket shopper can choose between 'hake steaks, hake centre cuts, hake tail pieces, hake fillets with skin, hake fillets without skin.' And what is not sold before its 'best before' date is presumably disposed of as part of the more than 30% of food thrown away each year in Britain,[1] and probably throughout Europe. Meanwhile, in Zimbabwe, UNICEF proclaims a massive food aid programme is needed because 5.5 million people face serious food shortages as a result of the regional drought and – we might add – the way our country is managed (or not).

Why are we having these famine-laden thoughts? Americans are fastidious about their health: the foods they eat, the calories and cholesterol they consume. But they still elect a president, George W. Bush, who refuses to face the big issue of the moment: global warming. Cutting down on gas emissions in the USA would be bad for the economy, he says. But there may be no economy for our grandchildren if we do not take climate change seriously.

---

1 *Guardian Weekly*, 22 April, 2005.

Perhaps the statistics and warnings that crowd in on us fatigue us. We sense that the world is a wearisome place, which yields reluctantly and painfully to change. Those who could make a difference to the lives of millions simply refuse to do so. They must know what is going on. The facts about hunger, poverty and disease are plain to see. Yet they do not raise a finger. They prefer to 'get on with their own lives,' even if it means fiddling while Rome burns.[2]

So we continue to struggle and die.

In the Harare Central Prison a man is pleading for help. He knows he could win an appeal against his sentence but he just cannot afford a lawyer to process it. So he remains in jail. In another part of the prison a man waits four years for his case to be heard. The judge dealing with his case has fled the country.

4 May, 2005

---

2   A reference to the Emperor Nero (54–68 AD) who preferred his pleasures to dealing with problems that arose, including the fire that destroyed much of Rome in the year AD64. Hence the expression 'fiddling while Rome burns'.

3

FISHY POLITICS

People are hungry. The government will accept outside help so
long as there are no political strings attached. 'The president
is very clear that whilst Zimbabwe welcomes drought-mitigating
assistance from other countries of good will, it remains firmly
opposed to any food handouts that are predicated on political
conditionalities.' Thus speaks George Charamba, presidential
spokesman, ostensibly unaware of the 'conditionalities' the
government itself imposes on the distribution of food. The
Zimbabwe *Standard* reports that MDC supporters in Zaka
'claim ZANU-PF officials, who control the distribution of grain
handouts, are denying them food as punishment for voting for
the opposition party in the 31 March parliamentary elections.'

Feeding the hungry unconditionally is surely the most basic
human duty. How an 'official' can turn away a starving person
defies belief. Yet the stories persist. People who have suffered
greatly over the past five years are now entering another phase
of deepening suffering as the winter approaches. Peter Henriot, a
Jesuit priest in Zambia, tells the modern parable of an imaginary
country where people were hungry. The country had many lakes
and rivers and bordered the sea.

The government decided that fishing was the answer to the
country's problems and a commission was set up to look into
ways of developing fishing. Donors were approached and they
provided funds for a study of the history of fishing. A report

was produced and launched in a hotel highly recommending the practice of fishing but no fish was on the menu as no one had done any fishing.

People of a theological bent decided to do a study of fishing in the Old Testament, using the books of Tobias [Tobit] and Jonah in particular. They found many convincing arguments in favour of fish and wrote study guides to make people aware of the benefits of fishing. But no one actually did any fishing.

Meanwhile the government decided to consult other countries in the region about their experiences of fishing and a team toured ten countries. (The start of the tour was delayed by disputes over travel allowances but this was finally resolved). While in these countries members of the team were invited to go fishing, but they declined because they were busy writing their report on the benefits these countries had found in fishing. On returning home they held seminars in hotels and tourist resorts around the country and came up with blueprints about developing fishing in the country, but no one actually went fishing.

A chair of Fishecology was set up at the national university but when time came for students to go on attachment they found there was nowhere to go, because...

16 May, 2005

4

A WITHERED LAND

There is a story in Mark's gospel about a man with a withered hand. It comes at the end of a series of incidents about the growing opposition to Jesus. The Pharisees watched him to see if he would cure the man on the Sabbath. Jesus 'looked angrily round at them, grieved to find them so obstinate,' (Mark 3:5). The Pharisees' main concern was not the man who was suffering but the threat Jesus posed to their power over the people. They saw him do a good thing – curing the man – and they immediately respond by plotting to destroy him.

This story is part of the tradition about Jesus and is written down some 40 years after it happened. In a time of extreme harassment of the Christians in Rome, they remembered the hostility that Jesus 'doing good'[1] produced in the chefs of that time who had no interest in the poor man with the withered hand. They just wanted to preserve their power.

So too in a stark way we face this puzzling fact about human nature. In a situation where something good is about to happen, people hold back and prefer the 'security' of no change, no challenge. Let everything continue as it is. We don't want this man coming in upsetting everything. We 'prefer the darkness to the light,' (John 3:19).

What kind of people are they who have no interest in a withered land but only want to preserve their own status? This

---

1   Acts 10:38

very week. truckloads of police have destroyed the livelihood of thousands of people who used to sell their wares at street comers to feed, clothe and school their families. These people would have worked in formal employment if they could find it. Instead they refused to just sit on their hands, but were determined to make some kind of living from vending. And what kind of response do they meet? Violence. We are told that hundreds, even thousands, have been arrested – for trying to help themselves.[2] And there are persistent reports that in the process a woman with a baby on her back was badly beaten and her baby died. Why are people doing this to one another? The land is dried out, the economy is flat and conscience has vanished. This is a dark, dark hour.

Africa Day, 2005

---

2   The total number of families directly affected by Murambatsvina was 700,000.

5

WHY?

People's houses and livelihoods are being destroyed a few kilometers from here. The action is being taken 'simply to clean up the city,' declares Resident Minister and Governor of Mashonaland East Province David Karimanzira. 'We will not stop at anything until we have achieved our goal,' said Harare Council spokesman, Leslie Gwindi. Seemingly they didn't 'stop at anything.' Morgan Tsvangirai, MDC leader, reported 'they didn't even have the heart to give people notice... (they) ploughed through (people's) properties and looted their goods.' One lady, bedridden with AIDS, was beaten because she did not move out fast enough nor pull down her one-roomed house fast enough in Hatcliffe Extension.

We are now asking one simple question. Why? If they really wanted to clean up the city why did they not distinguish between those who were, to use the President's own words, 'genuine players' and those who were criminals? Some, whose homes were destroyed were allocated plots by Housing Minister Ignatius Chombo in 2002 and have lease agreements. The World Bank and USAID provided water and other services. And why did they not first prepare the places where people are going to be moved to before destroying their present poor homes? Instead, Karimanzira said 'a committee under my office *will* soon find alternative places and land *will* be allocated to genuine house seekers.' (My emphases). What are people supposed to do in the winter cold meanwhile?

Eighteen thousand have been arrested so far and the government seems to feel very satisfied with itself. This self-satisfaction creates a fearful echo of the land invasions. Both come from the gut, not from the head. They arise from real anger at the defiance of the people – be they commercial farmers or city dwellers. These vengeful policies will lead us all ever deeper into misery. They defy all logic. They illustrate once again the obduracy, the blindness, the cruelty, the pride and selfishness of human beings.

And they have many antecedents. Three times in less than a dozen verses in John's gospel we hear Pilate say 'I find no case against him [Jesus],' (18:38, 19:4,6). He knew he was doing the wrong thing in condemning him and yet he went ahead and did it. He was afraid of the crowd, afraid of the emperor, afraid for his position – afraid of everything except his own conscience, which he simply ignored and smothered. Gut feelings, emotions, prompted his actions. Magnanimity, courage, justice and compassion – all were pushed aside.

Just now a first-hand report has come in from Hatcliffe Extension saying, 'the police are so intimidating.' The implication seems to be the police are not being themselves. They are intimidated and their only response is to intimidate others. How will they live with the knowledge of what they have done?

29 May, 2005

6

WAR ON THE POOR

'I have given up on this generation... I have given up on the people who were my friends, whom I played basketball with. It seems that they will never reckon with what they have done. But what I want is for their children to have a chance to make up their own minds. I want them to know and think about what happened, and learn from it.' Rwanda? Ivory Coast? Sudan? Actually, Bosnia. But it could have been any of them. And it could be Zimbabwe too. It expresses the utter helplessness and frustration of people who have been victims of overwhelming force and who yet do not give up, but look to the future. The speaker was Emir Suljagic, a Bosnian Muslim who survived the massacre of his people in Srebrenica ten years ago.[1] But he could have been anyone of the countless victims in countries where governments use violence against their own people.

We come once again to the age-old question – 'Who is my neighbour?' A simple harmless question but one that humanity refuses to face up to. The priest and the Levite in the story of the Good Samaritan (Luke 10: 25-3 7) have a briefcase full of reasons why they can't help. They are rushing to a meeting. It's not their job to look after such people. The victim could be a bait to trap a passerby and rob them too. Anyway, it is probably the victim's own fault. He is probably a totemless vagrant and not one of us.

The Samaritan just sees a human being in need. He is moved.

1   *Guardian Weekly*, May 20, 2005.

The Greek word is *splagnisthe* which means his whole insides turned over in compassion for the suffering person, so much so that he overcomes all the prejudices, all the baggage of history, all the fears that he could have listened to and acted on. It is an amazing story of breakthrough. It represents a huge step forward for humanity. But the story of the Good Samaritan remains the best-known gospel story precisely because it is so shocking, so attainable and yet at the same time so unattainable.

We are still dazed by the cruelty of our government in Zimbabwe who 'make war on the poor instead of on poverty.' But we continue to hope for a 'breakthrough' and that keeps us going. We wonder if we will ever see it from the tired old faces that haunt our TV screens and newspapers and we look to the young for change.

2 June, 2005

7

OUR HOMEGROWN TSUNAMI

It defies logic. It also defies belief. Even if you want to root out illegal traders and illegal homesteads, do you just bulldoze your way in without warrant and without warning; destroying not only houses and stores but a créche, a clinic and public toilets? Surely any government would first of all provide alternatives? This is winter. There are old people and young children now out in the open. They make a sort of laager with their few possessions in the open ground and they cook and sleep there. Everywhere there are good buildings knocked down. Children play on heaps of rubble. Some of this rubble is now flattened to meet up with the strip of tarmac but it is jagged and painful to walk on, especially at night, especially for small children. And the President flies off to Qatar.

Churches and NGOs are besieged with pleas for assistance to move belongings. They respond even though the government tries to block them from helping, even though they know in their anger that they are using scarce resources for a wholly unnecessary work. The government destroys and the churches and agencies have to respond. This is no time to struggle with the question 'why?'. People are hungry, cold and they have missed out on their anti-retroviral drugs. But the President doesn't seem to worry. He feels it's okay to fly off to Qatar.

The anger and incomprehension grows. The destruction goes on. The police are 'simply' restoring order. They are doing what they are told to do. This is no time to think about the future. 'I will have to live with this all my life. I should have disobeyed orders but I didn't. In my training I was told I need never obey an illegal order. But that was in training. This is the real thing. I can't stand out from others. So I knocked down the house of a widow, of a woman with AIDS. I turned children out into the cold. I ignored their cries. I destroyed the only livelihood of honest citizens. I was only doing what I was told to do. It is safer to obey orders.' Anyway the President has planned this. He knows best. Actually he is out of the country. He has gone to Qatar.

No one knows what to do. We shake our heads in disbelief. We laugh. We joke, 'is your house legal?'. It is our way of coping. To face the awfulness of it would be too much. I might get angry. I can't afford to be angry. They will beat me, even kill me if I get angry. Best just to stay quiet. I'll move away to the rural area even if there is no food there. That is what the President wants. He feels confident he will get his way. He is not worried. And anyway, he has gone to Qatar.

14 June, 2005

8

WALLS

In the courtyard of the former Plotzensee prison in Berlin there is a meditation in stone. It is made up of words and simple designs. The first word is Golgotha. Then comes Plotzensee itself, where political prisoners were hanged during the Nazi era. The next word is Auschwitz, the notorious extermination camp for Jews. Then Hiroshima in Japan where the atom bomb killed thousands, maybe hundreds of thousands of people. The final word is Walls. The meditation selects a few of the greatest tragedies in history to jolt us into thinking about our inhumanity to each other. And it ends with this simple word, 'walls.' Walls divide us one from another. They are an admission of failure built in stone.

The concept for the design of this meditation clearly came from the Berlin Wall built in 1960 to divide the city. The country, in fact all Europe, had already been divided by an 'iron curtain' some years before. The wall and the curtain lasted until 1989.

Edmund Burke a British historian once said 'those who do not know history are doomed to repeat it.' The Israelis, whose forebears died in Auschwitz, are now building a massive wall to protect themselves from the Palestinians. It seems incredible that a people with such a long history, who have nurtured some of the world's greatest thinkers – Einstein, for instance – should fail to see the pointlessness of an actual wall for preserving their long-term peace.

They must have built walls in their hearts long before they laid the first stone.

In Zimbabwe today, walls are being bulldozed and houses and livelihoods destroyed. But, ironically, it is the same process at work. As fast as walls of stone are knocked down new ones are going up in the hearts of those who ordered these acts. At a recent meeting between government ministers, church and NGO representatives in Zimbabwe there was a solid barrier against communication. The ministers simply refused to listen to those who described the suffering of the people. Instead, they dismissed the facts as 'unintended negatives', and continued to use the most extreme language about their own people, 95% of whom were only trying to make a living as best they could at a time of economic decline which, ironically, was of the government's own making.

'Father, forgive them: they know not what they do.'[1] These words, uttered on Golgotha, remain in force today. The invitation to reconciliation remains. 'As I live [it is the Lord Yahweh who speaks] I take pleasure, not in the death of a wicked man, but in the turning back of a wicked man who changes his ways to win life. Come back, come back, from your evil ways. Why are you so anxious to die ...?'[2]

21 June, 2005

---

1   Luke 23:34,
2   Ezekiel 33:11

9

INDEPENDENCE, YES. FREEDOM? NOT YET.

'From its declaration in 1991 Ukraine has enjoyed independence without freedom. Today it enjoys freedom.' So President Yushchenko summed up the events of December 2004. There is an atmosphere in Ukraine such that people know, however poor they are, that they can really build a better future starting now. There is a sudden confidence that no one will ever again exploit them and rob them of the fruits of their labour. The state and the structures of the state will, from now on, serve them, rather than the other way round.

One tries to enter into what it must mean to a country, which has never known freedom and which saw its lands torn apart by the tank battles of Soviets and Germans during the Second World War. Once the war was over, did people feel exhilarated or simply exhausted, despairing of the damage and the futility of so much destruction.

Zimbabwe lived through and was born of war, a war that has left a legacy not of hope, democracy, human rights and freedom, but of entitlement on the one hand; and of fighting all dissenting voices as if they were the enemy, on the other.

So sadly the exhilaration that many people enjoyed at Independence is not the experience of many young people today or of many young countries, Zimbabweans and Zimbabwe among them. Each day presents a new struggle to find work, transport and food, and now shelter. And all the time there is no security.

At any moment you may hear that your home and your livelihood have been destroyed. There have been countless testimonies these last weeks of people sitting among the ruins of their lives saying, 'I do not know what to do, I have no money, no food and nowhere to go.'

Each day we struggle with questions. We may try to banish the ugliest of answers, but they will not go away. Thirty years ago we also suffered. But then people knew what to look forward to: 'Rhodesia is the problem, Zimbabwe is the solution.' But seemingly 'Zimbabwe' was not the solution. Today many do not know what to do for their own lives neither do they know the way forward for the country. They are numb with shock and hopelessness. Joshua Nkomo wrote in the early 1980s, 'the hardest lesson of my life has come to me late. It is that a nation can win freedom without its people becoming free.'

Yet if there is one thing certain from the history of other parts of the world, it is that every people eventually bounce back like a branch disturbed by the passage of an elephant. You can finish the milk but soon it will be there again. *(Simba mukaka rinosinina.)* After thirteen chapters of indictment, the prophet Hosea, in his final chapter, records words of kindness for Israel: 'I will love them with all my heart, for my anger has turned from them, I will fall like dew on Israel. He shall bloom like the lily, and thrust out roots like the poplar, his roots shall spread far; he will have the beauty of the olive and the fragrance of Lebanon,' (14:5-7).

22 June, 2005

10

THE LASH GOES ON

In 1974 it seemed the impasse between our colonial settlers and freedom fighters would be settled within three years. 1977 came and went. A further three years of struggle and death had to go by before independence in 1980.

In 2000, when all hell broke loose in the country, who would have thought it would last five years? And it shows no signs of being over yet. Now we have had six weeks of Murambatsvina.[1] Protests from civic bodies, NGOs or churches make no difference. Voices from outside the country are not heeded. The cries of the people, their suffering and even their deaths make no difference to the authorities. The campaign of destruction and propaganda continues. There is a new word to soothe us – *garikai*, to be peaceful or safe. But words do not build houses or restore livelihoods. There is a hint now that the UN envoy, Minister Anna Tibaijuka from Tanzania, will not give a favourable report. So the media prepares for this by saying civic bodies and churches have hijacked her 'for their own political ends'. In war and times of civil strife, truth, it has been said, is the first victim. It is as though there is a deliberate policy of not listening to anything or anyone that questions the rightness of a policy long planned. This closedness when it comes to us is a most worrying development. 'My mind is made up. Do not confuse me with facts.' The Irish

---

1   Operation Murambatsvina meaning to 'clear out the rubbish', but also officially known as Operation restore order began i in June 2004.

poet, W. B. Yeats, who wrote 'things fall apart; the centre cannot hold;'[2] also wrote a short ironic poem, The Great Day, about the change of masters in his homeland after independence:

> *Hurrah for revolution and more cannon shot!*
> *A beggar upon horseback lashes a beggar on foot,*
> *Hurrah for revolution and cannon come again!*
> *The beggars have changed places, but the lash goes on.*

There is a lack of serious reflection about what we are doing to ourselves as a country. People are blindly obeying orders without, it seems, ever reflecting on the morality and long-term consequences of what they are doing. If history tells us anything, it is that there is always a reckoning – national and personal. You simply cannot trample on other people, or on your own conscience, without reaping a whirlwind sooner or later. The people most to be pitied in the long term are those who blindly co-operate in evil. They may have the whip hand and be on horseback but they remain beggars for they cannot earn our respect.

4 July, 2005

---

2   William Butler Yeats (1865-1939) The poem from which these lines are taken is 'The Second Coming written in 1919 in the aftermath of the First World War.

11

NO LONGER AT EASE

A cold coming we had of it,
Just the worst time of the year
For a journey, and such a long journey:
The ways deep and weather sharp,
The very dead of winter

And the night-fires going out, and the lack of shelters,
And the cities hostile and the towns unfriendly
And the villages dirty and charging high prices;
A hard time we had of it.
At the end we preferred to travel all night,
Sleeping in snatches,
With the voices singing in our ears, saying
That this was all folly...

The repeated 'and' in the middle of this extract from T. S. Eliot's 'Journey of the Magi' suggests an accumulation of woes as the wise men search for the new born king, Jesus. The poem describes a particular journey familiar to all who know the Christmas story. But it also describes a human experience repeated constantly in history: people on the move in search for a new way of life. The Magi did not have to set out on their journey in the middle of winter. We are not told that anyone had destroyed their 'illegal' dwellings or that they were 'criminal elements' involved in 'black market trading'. But, in another sense, they did have to set out.

They were caught up in a new hope for humanity. They had to set out, as Abraham did, 'without knowing where they were going,'[1] for the sake of all those who would follow them.

As I write, thousands of people in Zimbabwe are on the move. Many do not know where they are going. Their fathers came here for work in Federal times and they have no rural home to return to. Yes, Mr Gwindi, 'people came from somewhere' but so long ago that they do not now know from where. Even some of those who do have family in the rural areas are not being welcomed back. Relatives say, 'you are only remembering us now because you're in trouble.' Others move to relatives in town but giving rise to overcrowding and pushing up the price of rent. Others seek desperately to prove their dwellings are legal but they need fuel to go and fetch the plans. And there is no fuel – except for police vehicles and bulldozers. Some spend the night in the open 'for lack of shelter' and with 'night-fires going out', babies are dying of cold.

The accumulation of sorrows mount and worst of all is the feeling of helplessness. *The Zimbabwean* carried an appeal to Nelson Mandela recently to intervene. But that 'most gracious of men' – as the Queen of England called him in a Christmas broadcast – could well reply, 'my friend, who appointed me your judge, or the arbiter of your claims?'. (Luke 12:14) So we are thrown back on ourselves.

Eliot ends his poem:

> *I had seen birth and death,*
> *But had thought they were different; this Birth was*
> *Hard and bitter agony for us, like Death, our death.*
> *We returned to our places, these kingdoms,*
> *But no longer at ease here, in the old dispensation...*

13 July, 2005

---

1   Hebrews ll:8

12

TOTALLY ALONE

'He went into the bush to find wood, but when he returned he found that a distant relative had arrived and taken his young brother and sister away. He is now all alone in the world. As he stares into the crackling fire, his only companion, tears run down his cheeks.' This extract from a news report on Caledonia Farm tells of a 17-year-old orphan moved there from Hatcliffe when his small home was bulldozed and burnt by the government. We are already saturated with information about Murambatsvina even before UN envoy Tibaijuka gives her verdict. We have asked the simple question 'why?' for two months and had no answers. Or rather, if we received an answer, it only posed a further question.

Could we just go back for a moment over the years? **1980:** Euphoria; Independence at last. **1982:** Pride and elation as schools, clinics and opportunities abound. **1985:** Bewilderment as the truth of Gukurahundi leaks out and violent retribution is visited on the few in Mbare who vote against the government. **1988:** Unity accord but no truth and reconciliation. Economy slows. **1991:** ESAP; retrenchments and gradual withdrawal of support for social services. **1995:** Unreality as opposition melts away in the election. 1997: Un-budgeted pay-outs to war-veterans. Inflation quickens. **1999:** A sense of hope as civil society comes together to propose alternative ways forward. **2002:** Government responds to opposition by tearing down the economy and reducing people to queuers. **2005**: Further destruction; this time of people's homes together with promises that new ones will be built 'possibly as early as 2010'.

What is one to make of these swings between joys and sorrows, hope and despair? Living in the midst of it must be not unlike living in the desert all those years ago. 'What good have you done us, bringing us out of Egypt? We spoke of this in Egypt, did we not? Better to work for the Egyptians than to die in the wilderness.' (Exodus 14:11) Forty years they had of it and even then God was 'weary' of them (Psalm 95). 'Their hearts are astray. These people do not know my ways.'

Can we glean hope from our present experience? Can we say that we are in a process? A process of healing? *Kuseka nhamo, kunge rugare*: to laugh at troubles brings peace. People have a wonderful ability to laugh when things are really bad. To laugh is to somehow recognise that we are ultimately powerless to heal ourselves though we have to do what we can. But there is One who can heal. Sometimes he doesn't do it in a day – or even in 25 years. We are out of Egypt, for sure. But are we in the promised land? It's like the two little girls who wanted to ride a pony. They went to the stable but all they found was horse manure. One little girl cried but the other one laughed and said, 'with all this shit around there must be a pony.'

19 July, 2005

13

I DON'T WANT TO SEE YOU HERE

'I don't want to see you here on Monday.' These words of a police officer to a person transported to Caledonia Farm in the recent Murambatsvina rang in my ears all weekend. The man's home was bulldozed, his livelihood ruined and he was removed. Now, after a few weeks in the open, he is simpy told to go and he knows the consequences if he does not comply. So he comes to ask for help. One cannot refuse someone in great need but the assistance is given with implicit anger because it is so unnecessary. The victim's suffering was not the result of a natural disaster such as drought or locusts. It was man-made, and deliberate.

We are getting tired of speaking and writing about the relentless government campaign against its own people. In the search for understanding the word that keeps coming is 'rejection.' The people have rejected us so we will reject the people. They are not the people we want. The playwright Bertolt Brecht wrote of the communist government in East Germany after the rising in 1953, 'it is dissolving the people and creating a new one'.

We can draw sinister conclusions from present events. We know about genetic engineering, which radically modifies seeds and how they interact with their environment. Similarly, we are now seeing social engineering, which seems to be an attempt to create a compliant people, molded to behave in the way Big Brother wants. Perhaps we have not left 1984 behind us after all.

It won't work, of course; people aren't seeds. They modify according to their environment but they do it by choice. You can browbeat and condition some people some of the time, like our police friend above, but you can't do it to all the people all the time. It is not a permanent solution. So why even attempt it? The answer to this question leads us into such dark motives that it might be better to move on and remember the Book Fair.

Yes, the Book Fair. Last night two hundred people crowded into a room in the Monomotapa, (why do they always underestimate numbers?), for the official opening. The former speaker of the South African Parliament spoke passionately about the duty of writers to 'meet the people's needs'. She recalled that African writers flourished in the decades that embraced independence but that later African governments felt threatened and writers found themselves in prison or exile. She felt that ten years into independence in South Africa, writers were failing to respond to the expectations of the people. What of Zimbabwe? The evening opened with two serious but hilarious poems, which among other things called us a nation of queuers. The house erupted in laughter.

No, we are not going to be manipulated.

3 August, 2005

14

A TALE OF TWO CITIES

Harare is two cities and Zimbabwe is two countries. Avondale shopping centre car park is full. Where do the vehicles come from? And where do their owners find fuel? We have an economy that seems to suit some people just fine. They make their money and buy their goods. They seem unconcerned that there is another city.

But there is another city where people are hammered daily. Their houses have been destroyed and are crowded in with relatives or they have gone to rural areas where there is no food. Even those who own legal houses have been slapped with fines. No wonder they would love to leave if they could. People did not rush to the book fair or the agriculture show. If you want to see crowds you just have to go to the South African Embassy.

Some years ago a Brazilian politician remarked of his own country, 'the economy is going well, but the people are suffering'. The economy is that whole interrelationship of goods and services which enables people to survive. It is the first concern of a government to make it work. Yet looking at the most recent action of our government we see legislation that (i) creates a senate,[1] (ii) removes the right of citizens to appeal to the courts in certain cases,[2] and (iii) denies some people the right to travel when they have been denied a passport on the basis that they

---

1   The resuscitation of the Upper House took place in 2005.

2   This pertained to the constitutional amendment which removed the right to appeal from the Administrative Court's adjudication over compensation arising from land seizures.

have no right to citizenship.[3] What have these measures to do with getting the economy moving? In the 1980 general election the present ruling party came out with its manifesto declaring:

> ZANU-PF believes that the common interests of the people are paramount in all efforts to exploit the country's resources, that the productive processes must involve them as full participants in both decision-making processes, management and control.

I treasured this pamphlet for many years. It set out an idealistic agenda for a government of the people and I longed for its realisation.

But the reverse has happened. Economists tell us people are worse off now than they were 25 years ago. True, in 1980, the government offered opportunities to people who had been denied them. They also made great efforts to extend health and education services to all citizens, but they didn't do anything to show they really believed that 'the common interests of the people are paramount,' still less to 'involve them as full participants'. Decisions continued to be made at the top as they were in Rhodesian days.

Now here we are, 25 years on, but rather than building on the aspirations of the poor – we seem intent on taking away even the little they have and denying them the choice to decide on matters that concern them – a tenet enshrined in the manifesto of 1980.

31 August, 2005

---

3   In 1984, the government passed a Citizenship Act, which outlawed dual citizenship. If one was a dual citizen and wanted to retain Zimbabwean citizenship, one had to renounce any foreign citizenship. Subsequently a Citizenship Amendment Bill tightened up rules in order to strip Zimbabweans who had been out of the country of their citizenship. Thirdly, in the 2000s, the ruling party feared the prospect of Zimbabweans in the diaspora being able to claim citizenship and vote; and they wanted to disenfranchise many farmworkers – often of Mozambican or Malawian parentage – whom they believed voted with the white farmer and for the opposition. Thus, the citizenship laws were tightened again and in order to claim Zimbabwean citizenship one had to renounce any theoretical claim one might have to citizenship in another country, which was often very difficult to do.

15

CHOLERA AND CURTAINS

For some days our attention has been on curtains. *The Herald's* front page carries the headline, 'NO TO CITY'S EXTRAVAGANZA' referring to a government veto on the Harare City Council's plan to spend $35 billion on furniture and curtains for the mayor's mansion. Inside, since today is St Valentine's Day, a cartoon suggests the proposed curtains should be red.

The front page article goes on to quote a Dzivarasekwa resident, Thomas Mukumbati, as protesting, 'in terms of priorities, what makes sense? We are busy warding off flies and we have to endure the smell of raw sewage when someone wants to spend money on furniture. At the end of the day we think we are not people. The council only needs our rates and not us.'

Then we turn to page 2 and see Mukumbati's point: the continuing story of the unhygienic handling of food in Epworth, which was responsible for the death from cholera of five people over the weekend in Domboramwari.

But 'hold on' we say. *The Herald* is telling us that the city mayor (appointed by the government) proposes to spend vast sums of money from *our* rates on *her* residence. And Mukumbati, who lives in the high densities, complains that council policies are so demeaning that the residents are no longer regarded as people. But both the curtains and the cholera are due directly or indirectly to government decisions. Why then are they reported in a government-controlled paper, *The Herald*? Is the intention to suggest that 'we are really on your side'? If Mr Mukumbati had joined with others to march down Second Street protesting at the city's priorities he would probably now be languishing behind bars with the brave WOZA women. Instead he has just been given prime coverage in *The Herald*.

It amounts to saying, 'we know there are many things wrong but we are not prepared to do anything about them. We are, however, prepared to air them so that you can feel the government really cares. That should take some of the steam out of your anger and let us off the hook for a little longer.'

Shifting the blame is an old game. The Hebrews did it when they got 'the goat to bear all their faults away with it into a desert place' (Leviticus 16:22). Scapegoating has always been easy.

17 February, 2006

16

WATCHING IN ANGUISH

'Armed police at the weekend raided a squatter camp on the banks of Mucheke river in Masvingo city, burnt down the plastic shacks and chased away more than 200 people including children who lived at the camp. The squatters, who watched in anguish as their shacks and belongings went up in smoke, had lived at the illegal camp since about 2001... the demolition comes barely a week after President Robert Mugabe promised during his 18 April Independence Day speech to continue demolishing illegal settlements, to smash crime and to restore the beauty of Zimbabwe's cities and towns.' So ran a news report on the 26th April 2006.

And so we continue our daily life in Zimbabwe. It is not just the squatters who watch suffering. It seems nothing touches the hearts of those who order and carry out these acts. At a time when inflation is rocketing and people's lives are becoming more unbearable by the hour all the government can think of is to continue its cruel demolition of people's lives. Force used on the helpless just goes on and on. Do we not have eyes to see the pain and ears to hear the cries? Or is it that those in authority have simply hardened their hearts and persuaded themselves that all their actions are justified for some distant goal, conjured up by a tiny unaccountable minority for their own purposes. One can persuade oneself of anything if you try hard enough. Amy Tan offers this parable in her book *Saving Fish From Drowning*:

A pious man explained to his followers: 'It is evil to take lives and noble to save them. Each day I pledge to save a hundred lives. I drop my net in the lake and scoop out a hundred fishes. I place my fish on the bank where they flop and twirl. "Don't be scared," I tell those fishes, "I am saving you from drowning". Soon enough the fishes grow calm and lie still. Yet, sad to say, I am always too late. The fishes expire. And because it is evil to waste anything, I take those dead fishes to market and I sell them for a good price. With the money I receive, I buy more nets so I can save more fishes.'

It is so painful, day after day, to hear and read about the suffering of our fellow Zimbabweans. It is so hard to understand why a government, which claims to be elected by the people for the people, does this. Blaise Pascal (1623-62) wrote, 'Jesus will be in agony even to the end of the world.' He looked for comfort from his disciples in Gethsemane and found none. And so it has always been. Those by the Mucheke river also look for comfort but find nought.

1 May, 2006

17

IVAN THE TERRIBLE

The first tsar of Russia ruled with ferocious cruelty for almost 40 years (1547-84). Ivan earned the sobriquet, 'the Terrible,' due to his obsession with retaining his life and his power through violence. And he had the support of a section of the Russian population that 'admired a leader' who, in the words of James Meek, a recent reviewer[1] of a new book on Ivan 'frightened troublemakers, bandits and ne'er-do-wells –so long as those punished remained comfortably remote.' One way Ivan had of surviving was to divide the country in two, 'unleashing one – the part he took for his own – to prey murderously, greedily and destructively on the other.'

These words stayed with me as I read on the Kubatana website Professor Tony Hawkins' lecture, 'Still Standing: The economic, political and security situation in Zimbabwe 2006 and implications for the SADC region'. Hawkins addresses the question so many of us ask: how is it that with an economic decline that has cut GDP by 40% and halved income per head, Zimbabwe still survives? His answer is that a privileged elite has discovered its interests are best served by maintaining the status quo. They are quite happy with a divided country. So there are now two Zimbabwe's: this small elite who have 'captured' the state and milk it and the huge majority of the people who struggle day in and day out to simply survive. There is no 'middle class' to speak of. The professionals

---

1   *London Review of Books* 27:23, 1/12/05.

– teachers, doctors, nurses, public servants – have either joined the low-income group or have emigrated. Hawkins sees the one underlying explanation for our 'fade-away' as 'the paramountcy of political survival.' The government doesn't govern. It uses all its waking hours shoring up its own hold on power.

The choice that faces us is clear. We either choose democracy, pluralism and openness or we accept even greater repression. And this latter course raises all sorts of questions about why. The answers are manifold. Fear, certainly; apathy, yes, for different reasons; a fond expectation that other people in the opposition will take the flack and fight the battle for you; and God. How many people have turned to churches of all kinds – it itself a huge issue – to pray that God will do everything for them, salvation with neither commitment nor action. At the moment we are choosing fear and apathy. It is just conceivable that intense economic realities will eventually force the government to change course.' But how long is 'eventually?'

I know that taking a cue from the British is now out of fashion but when Alec Douglas Home was chosen over Rab Butler as Prime Minister in the 1960s, someone congratulated his mother over her son's success. 'I think Butler would have been a better choice,' she is said to have replied. The story illustrates the call to put the country first before any personal ambition. Now, there's openness for you.

17 May, 2006

18

WHAT VALUES ARE THESE?

Again and again I find I return to the effort to understand. Why, for example, do the authorities in this country not care about the suffering of the people? The hardships people now endure are extensively documented. No one can claim they don't know what is going on. Yet those who could change the situation do nothing or else they journey across the globe seeking help while the solution lies in front of them at home.

Why do we behave like this? What do our present actions, or lack of action, tell us about our values? I have heard it said that our strongest motivation is the preservation of social relations. What gives me security is the sense of belonging to a group, and for a few this also means leading that group and nourishing its cohesion through perks and protection: in a word, patronage. Anything that challenges that cohesion has to be confronted and subdued. There is nothing of more value than this cohesion. In fact adhering to its bonds can be a matter of life or death.

Notions like being 'subject to the law', 'respect for property', even 'human rights' – all these become useful only insofar as they serve the basic value of social cohesion as understood by me. Is it wrong for me to get my passport through the efforts of my brother-in-law who works at the passport office? For goodness sake, what a question! If you don't 'know' people somewhere in the system you will not have a happy life.

Social cohesion is a good value and has deep roots. It is what has protected people from harm for millennia. But it is exclusive; it depends on a 'them' and 'us' mentality. When Margaret Thatcher was about to meet someone she did not know she would first ask, 'is he one of us?' So, paradoxically, the pursuit of social cohesion is divisive when it considers only one group. What has bogged down any progress in the national project in Zimbabwe since 1980 is the constant harping on 'enemies within.' Instead of building an inclusive society where all are welcome – and Growth with Equity, that credo of the early 1980s,[1] really is a value – we have blamed and excluded everyone available: whites, PF-ZAPU, 'puppet' oppositions, 'totemless aliens,' whites (again), the NGOs, the private schools, even Blair and Bush[2] (although they are hardly 'within').

It is accepted that political parties decide policies, but who decides values? The clear answer must be 'the people'. And that must mean all the people, including the Venda and the vendors. To build on exclusivity and division is to build on sand.

4 June, 2006

---

1   See also http://www.ijhssnet.com/journals/Vol_2_No_8_Special_Issue_April_2012/26.pdf
2   Tony Blair the prime minister of the UK 1997-2007; George Bush, president of the USA 2001-09.

19

DYING

'**Z**imbabwe is the most unhappy country in the world!' – so says a study reported on the BBC today[1] (Vanuatu, in the Pacific, seemingly, is the happiest). Readers of *The Zimbabwean* will be familiar with the reasons for our grading but among them is the relentless pressure of funerals.

But, of course, first comes the dying and why people die today is not only physically painful but emotionally too. Gone is the normal way of departing surrounded by relatives most of whom will be younger than the dying person. Often it is parents burying their own adult sons and daughters. But to me the saddest of all is those who die alone, unsupported, even abandoned. They have a solitary struggle with their emotions.

Elizabeth Kübler-Ross[2] taught us about dying. She said that often people go through painful mental stages before they are ready to leave this world. When they first discover they have cancer or AIDS or some other terminal illness their first reaction is often denial. 'It can't be true. The doctors will find a remedy. There's this treatment you can get in...'

When they realise the diagnosis *is* correct, they get angry. Angry with life, with others, whomever they can blame, and often angry with God. It is a deep frustration to feel my life is to be cut

1   13 July, 2006.
2   Elizabeth Kübler-Ross, a Swiss psychiatrist, wrote a book called *On Death and Dying* in which she suggested five stages of grief: denial, anger, bargaining, depression and, finally acceptance.

off. I will no longer be able to fulfill my plans, see my children grow – to say nothing of my grandchildren. A way out of anger is to bargain. Again God comes into it at this third stage. 'If I get better, I will change my ways. I promise, I will do this and that...'

But soon real frustration sets in when it becomes clear this bargaining line is not yielding results. This is the point when anger can return and turn into deep depression, and a moment when a person really needs to be accompanied because this must be the loneliest journey of all. But, as we say, the greatest darkness is just before dawn. And this is the moment when the dying person can move into acceptance, peace, and even happiness.

We buried one of our priests today. He struggled for months and weeks with growing enfeeblement. Recently the doctor told him he had no more than a week left. When someone called to see him some days ago, Fr Willie said cheerfully, 'just three days to go!' He was surrounded by friends, nurtured by his faith, and reconciled to death. But what of those who die alone?

13 July, 2006

20

INHABITING TWO WORLDS

Bishop Alexio Muchabaiwa once talked about the frog in a sermon in Triashill, near Rusape. When the going gets rough on land the frog jumps into the water and swims around for a bit. But if there is a lot of turbulence in the water it quickly retreats back onto dry land. The bishop concluded we too live in two worlds. We try to escape from one when the going is tough and look for comfort elsewhere. He was referring to Christians who keep one foot in traditional religion and the other in the church. But his parable could equally apply elsewhere.

Take Chinhoyi, for example. Recently the President came to the consecration of the new bishop and after the ceremony was over he addressed the large crowd. He was extremely warm and relaxed as he retraced his own Catholic background and upbringing at Kutama. He clearly has great respect, even affection, for the church and once again expressed his desire for co-operation with her. The people enjoyed his words, laughed at his jokes and applauded him.

Yet the listener could not help wondering. Are these gracious words coming from the same person who has led this government this past six years? This is a government that has violently confiscated the land of farmers, destroyed the houses and businesses of town people and presided over the fastest decline of any economy on the continent. Many people are short of food, medicines, shelter, school fees, work, freedom to meet and freedom to express their views.

How is it possible to switch off one world and live in another? How is it possible to be so friendly, courteous and winning on the one hand and yet so 'vicious' – a word he himself used at a recent prayer meeting – on the other? We know from history that there are many examples. There is film footage showing Hitler being charming with children. It is true, a person can be tough at one time and gentle at another yet one senses there is no disharmony in their character. But sometimes a person behaves now in one way, now in another, and we sense there is a complete contradiction between the two. We find ourselves back in Ezekiel's time among the 'prophets who have empty visions and give lying predictions ... they have misled my people by saying: Peace! when there is no peace' (Ezek 13: 9).

To be or not to be a person of integrity! That is Hamlet's question to Zimbabweans today. To live by my convictions no matter what the consequences: Can we do that?

3 September, 2006

21

AUTHORITY DISTORTED

Authority, the dictionary tells us, comes from author, which itself comes from the Latin word 'augere', to increase, to grow. So someone in authority is there to help people to grow, to find their way. Authorities are there to open the way for people to grow and develop their gifts. The scriptures are scathing about those who abuse their authority by thinking only of their own growth and power: 'trouble for the shepherds of Israel who feed themselves! Shepherds ought to feed their flock' (Ezekiel 34:2). 'Their so-called rulers make their authority felt. This is not to happen among you. Anyone who wants to become great among you must be your servant' (Mark 10:42).

An author is usually considered to be someone who has written something original, like a book. But it applies also to every creative activity that moves our life forward. The desire to create is very basic. Children play with wire or clay and come up with the most ingenious products. As we grow older the desire to create becomes ever stronger. It is a life-force that pushes people to sacrifice much in order to study, or start a business or build a home. Since 'authors' can clash with one another in the pursuit of their creativity they have ceded part of their authorship to 'authorities' – people who will respect individuals' rights to be creative while at the same time making sure that others' rights are not infringed.

All very theoretical! But it provides a basis for reflecting on the ongoing effects of Murambatsvina. That 'tsunami' swept away people's homes and livelihoods over a year ago. But still to this day there are people without proper shelter who are continually living under the fear of having the revival many have attempted again swept away. Recent reports indicate that many people in Mbare (perhaps 46%) are now suffering from mental illness caused by the stress under which they live. It is not hard to see why. A person is struggling to find food, rent, school fees and then is hit by deaths in the family due to the 'great sickness'. Day and night they worry about how long they can continue like this.

'Authorities,' whose only justification for being there is to facilitate the growth of people, have ended up being the very ones who frustrate that growth. There are too many accounts of bureaucracy and delays in public offices and services and of demands for bribes for us to be in any doubt that society has been infected by a cruel distortion of the very structure it is supposed to be. We do not live in an 'enabling' society but one where every attempt at creativity is thwarted. Authority has lost its meaning.

23 October, 2006

22

TIED UP IN KNOTS

The French have a word for it – *denouement*. Literally it is the untying (of knots). It has come to mean the final act in a drama where the truth comes out and a new reality emerges. Are we moving towards this in our seven-year drama? For Paul it happened at Damascus. The whole false thrust of his life fell apart and a new life opened before him. Many of us as individuals have had such moments. 'It changed my life,' we say. It can be a moment of extraordinary liberation and give us new energy.

Something like this happened in the life of the scientist, Richard Feynman, who worked at 'humble' problems in physics and eventually was awarded a Nobel Prize in 1965. He hated the prospect of the formal ceremony of receiving the prize and the 'snobbery associated with kings' but was 'loosened' by the welcome in Stockholm, Sweden. 'The Prize,' he wrote, 'was a signal to permit [friends, relatives, students and colleagues] to express, and me to learn about, their feelings ... For this I thank Alfred Nobel and the many... and you, Swedish people, with your honours and your trumpets and your king – forgive me. For I understand at last - such things provide entrance to the heart.'

It happens to individuals. It can also happen to countries and maybe the whole planet?

England in 1950 was a grim place. Scarred and exhausted by war, blackened by the smoke of factories and with its grey sky ever-laden with rain, it seemed to be trapped in decline. Then a moment came - the accession of a Queen – and new energy flowed. Public buildings were cleaned up and smog (smoke + fog) was outlawed. Today we have climate warming. Again there is a sense of hopelessness. Who will loosen the knots we tie ourselves in? We await our Damascus.

And so to Zimbabwe! We are tied up in knots. No one seems to know how to undo them. We await something: some dawn of understanding, some moment of conversion. In the second century Irenaeus[1] wrote, 'the knot of Eve's disobedience was untied by Mary's obedience'. Mary was faced with the choice of remaining secure in her own little world of Nazareth or of opening herself to God in an incredible act of trust. We know what she chose and for two thousand years have reflected on her 'yes'. She untied the knot not only for Eve but for us all. The Germans even give her the title of Knotenloserin, the one who unties knots.

I met a man at the weekend who was burdened by family problems. 'I can't even think straight,' he said. He needed someone to think for him and with him, someone to untie his knots. That's how we, as a people, are in Zimbabwe today but do we really want someone to loosen our knots or can we not even make the effort to try?

14 November, 2006

---

1   Irenaeus, who died c. AD 202, is also referred to as Saint Irenaeus. He was Bishop of Lugdunum in Gaul, then a part of the Roman Empire (now Lyon, France). An early Church Father and apologist, his writings were formative in the early development of Christian theology.

23

AN ENTRANCE

There is a scene in the film about the Grand Duchess Anastasia where the members of the Russian Royal family suddenly enter a ballroom and we hear the duchess say, 'I do so love an entrance!' Indeed an 'entrance' is what we often wait for: the teams to appear on the football pitch, the singer to appear on the stage or a politician to appear at a rally. The excitement comes from the expectation of some moving experience we will have.

But what if the 'appearance' is a moment of judgment? The one who appears comes to make a decision that will affect our lives. For that, there is apprehension, not excitement. For many days people have been talking about the 'Gono issue' by which they mean which way will the chairman of the Reserve Bank jump? Will he devalue or not? In the event he entered and he left and nothing changed. Some say it was a political decision not an economic one. He was not going to do the orthodox thing and be seen to bow to the IMF and 'the west'. Others say he is waiting to introduce the new currency and that would somehow solve the problem. Whatever the reason, his 'entrance' seems to have left us just where we were before.

The Christian cycle of feasts about the manifestation of the Messiah that started with Christmas and ends with Candlemas on 2 February.[1] This celebration, forty days later, marks the moment when Jesus 'suddenly enters' (Malachi 3:1) the temple in Jerusalem. It is a moment that deeply affects an old man who had waited all his life for this 'entrance'. Simeon rejoices to see the 'light of the nations' finally come, but he also knows that his coming will mean a time of decision; 'he is destined for the fall and the rising of many' (Luke 2:28).

After all the waiting, all the yearning for things to change, a decisive instant will come. Important decisions, either personal or national, cannot be put off indefinitely. The longer we try to postpone them the more painful the inevitable results will be. When tough decisions have to be made it is best to face them. Whether it is Bush in Iraq, Gono in the Reserve Bank or any one of us facing a painful truth about our situation, a moment will come which will give a worse result than the one we would have had if we had grasped the moment in time.

2 February, 2007

---

1   Candlemas is a Christian holiday celebrated annually on 2 February. It celebrates three occasions according to Christian belief: the presentation of the child Jesus; Jesus' first entry into the temple; and it celebrates the Virgin Mary's purification (mainly in Catholic churches).

24

A PEAK EXPERIENCE

A shot from 25 yards goes soaring past the defenders into the top left corner of the net; a tennis serve bullets into the comer of the box leaving the receiver totally wrong-footed. Peak experiences come in different sizes but they all describe a moment of exhilaration when a person is beyond themselves with joy. It could be in sport, in music or just in ordinary life. Someone experiences something on a journey, cooking a meal or getting out of bed in the morning.

A radio interviewer once told Karl Rahner, a renowned Catholic theologian of the twentieth century, that he had never had an experience of God. 'I don't believe you,' responded Rahner emphatically. 'You have had no experience of God under this precise code-word God, but you have had or have now an experience of God – and I am convinced that this is true of every person.'

The writers of the first three gospels all mention an incident in the life of Jesus where a veil is briefly lifted. (The writer of the fourth gospel doesn't have to mention this event as his whole gospel serves this purpose). The incident is when Jesus takes three of his closest companions – Peter, James and John – up a mountain and he appears to them as utterly transformed. 'As he prayed, the aspect of his face was changed and his clothing became brilliant as lightening' (Luke 9:29). Then Peter spoke to Jesus: 'Lord,' he said 'it is wonderful for us to be here' (Matt

17:4). But a moment later it was all over. 'They looked around and saw no one except Jesus.'

In the dynamic of the gospel story we understand this brief revelation was to prepare the disciples for the scandal of the Passion. It didn't. When the Passion came they all fled and when Peter did manage to come back to 'see what would happen' (Matt 26:58) he ended up swearing three times that he knew nothing about the man. It was only years later, long after the truth had really sunk in, that Peter speaks of the glory 'we had seen for ourselves... when we were with him on the holy mountain' (2 Peter 1:16 -18).

It is a sad thing, but often peak experiences don't seem to really make a difference. Hearing Prime Minister Elect, Robert Mugabe, dressed in a white suit, speak on the Rhodesian TV about reconciliation and the future on the eve of independence, 1980, was, for this writer, a peak experience. Together with so many others I was exhilarated. But today, 'years later,' what has happened to my 'peak experience'? It is in tatters.

2 March, 2007

25

DARKNESS OVER THE LAND

It is Good Friday and Matthew tells us 'there was darkness over all the land'. This is the climax of the 'work' of Jesus. There is a sense of anguish and despair. Even the disciples who 'had hoped' (Luke 24:21) had given up and left.

A neighbouring leader has likened Zimbabwe's economic crisis to the Titanic, saying that its citizens are being forced to leave 'like passengers jumping from the sinking ship to save their lives'.[1] Those that remain struggle, or have their heads in the air refusing to acknowledge that there is a problem or blaming other people for it. So we continue on our divided way while our country ploughs ever deeper into the mire.

I met a man the other day who told me that he was simply walking home to his house after work when he was set on by police, taken to their station, robbed of his money and cruelly assaulted. He lay on the floor for the night and next morning was simply told 'you can go now'.

There is darkness over the land. At this point the person of faith may jump in and say, 'Ah, but then there was Easter and the light shone in the darkness.' Yes, it is true but this cannot trip from our lips like a blanket covering a tortured victim. Easter is no magic wand, no cheap respite. We utterly evacuate its meaning if we speak of the resurrection lightly.

Jesus entered deeply into the human experience of greed, spite, jealousy, hypocrisy, power, wealth, lies, cowardice, betrayal,

---

1   Levy Mwanawasa, BBC News, 21/03/07.

torture and death. This was a terrible path which the Son of Man trod. He 'set his face like flint' (Isaiah 50:7) to walk that path 'ahead of us' (John 10:4) and 'for us' (Luke 22:19). The resurrection was a breakthrough after a long endurance.

It is *the* victory in human history, dwarfing every cup final and liberation victory, and its message embraces 'everyone' (Acts 2:38).

6 April, 2007

26

A NERVOUS DISPOSITION

'Government therefore calls upon the peace-loving flock and other well-meaning clergymen to ignore the programme of prayer meetings that are called for in the pastoral letter.' So ends the almost full-page critique in *The Herald* about the Catholic Bishops' recent letter. The 'therefore' refers to the argument that during prayer people actually mention the things that are troubling them and this mere description of the pain they are suffering is described as 'unforgivable' and 'anti-government'.

We have known for some time that our government is nervous of any free expressions of opinion whether on the air-waves or in print or in public meetings. But now it seems they are nervous about prayer. Yet prayer by its nature reaches beyond human boundaries and is the one human activity that cannot be criminalised. Thought too is beyond the reach of the law – though George Orwell, in *1984*, parodied a scenario in which the 'Thought Police' tried to control it. However fanciful it might seem, many governments, including our own, try to control the thoughts of their citizens. And if you have control of media, this is not very difficult to do.

An extraordinarily interesting event has just taken place in Northern Ireland. Though the British first attempted to colonise Ireland in the twelfth century it was only in the seventeenth that they made a concerted effort to stamp out 'rebellion' and settle the country. They succeeded in the north to such an extent that when the Irish eventually won independence, in the twentieth century, the majority of people in the north, which is largely Protestant, vehemently refused to own the freedom gained by the south, which is largely Catholic. A seething resentment simmered for decades until the civil rights movement in the USA blew the top off 'the North' in the late 1960s. Twenty-five years of hatred and violence boiled over and it has only been in the last thirteen years that a painful step-by-step process of first toleration and then reconciliation has emerged. The process has involved countless people examining themselves, asking 'is this endless confrontation and conflict what I really want?' These people have slowly learnt to respect the other side; they have tried to understand them and listen to them. A few weeks ago we saw a picture of the two leaders – each representing the extremes of Northern Irish politics, sitting at the same table. It was almost laughable that the journalist added 'there was no handshake.' Who cares about the detail of a handshake if people have managed to put eight hundred years of bitter history to rest?

But, without question, this reconciliation would have been impossible without prayer on all sides. Prayer enables us to transcend our petty, selfish, narrow biases. We will get nowhere without it. But we will get a long way with it. That our government should want to ban prayer seems to suggest that they are simply not interested in reconciliation or in the truth of people's lived experiences.

28 April, 2007

27

THE BOAT CLUB

A few boats lie turned over on the grass by the lake; a single yacht is beached on dry land. A few fishermen and women wile away the day catching small fry on the decaying pier. The wood is rotting on the look-out structures. The huge club house, with its rows of tables, its lounge and bar, is locked up and the swimming pool abandoned. A shield on the wall gives the names of the chairmen back to 1938. Come 1998 and there is an empty space. A faded colour photo has the caption: 'Cape to Rio race, 1972.'

It takes little imagination to people the place. Let's say it's 1960. Men and boys busy about boats. Women chatting and preparing *braais* and children swimming in the pool or running wild all over the place. 'These people knew how to build places of relaxation.' Yes, they did. But they built them for themselves. Other people, who were a bit different, even if they were teachers and lawyers and wealthy bus owners, could not go there. And because there was no sharing, no open doors, no welcome, there was no continuity. Why keep up something you were never part of? So the club slips into decay. Maybe someone will rescue it but it won't be for boats. Maybe some students will come for courses or worn out clerics will use it as a rest house.

The tragedy of our country is deep-seated. So many missed opportunities. So many wrong turnings. Those who carved out the railways and built the bridges; those who laid out the farms and game reserves, hospitals and schools, and institutions of governance all had vision and worked hard. But the poison of selfish exclusivity as there from the beginning. We build for ourselves, and those others insofar as they serve us. This philosophy, this fundamental world view, infected every aspect of life.

The people who practiced this way of life are different now but their attitude endures. And what is worse, today they do not have the desire to make the country work, as the earlier 'bosses' did. The Rhodesian certainly wanted a good life for themselves but in the process everyone benefited to some extent: there were no power cuts, no water shortages. The railways worked efficiently, the country's finances were controlled – one R$ equalled two US$ at Independence. Then, as now, there was indifference to those who were not 'one of us' but there were few cases of looting of public assets for private purposes.

Our country still has people who say, 'all this is for me and mine. You others can fend for yourselves. It is of no concern to me if you have no water and no electricity, if your roads are pot-holed, and your children suffering from kwashiorkor, or there are no books in your schools. We can drink to our success at the golf club, congratulate ourselves on our newfound wealth, the latest deal we've made, and our latest purchase.'

Today, beyond the cheering and the gloating, there is emptiness and pain. The owners of the club have changed, the selfishness and the exclusivity endures.

31 May, 2007

28

THE GRASS IS BURNING

We are in the season of burnt grass. People hunt animals by destroying their habitat and forcing them into the open. I have never discovered how successful this practice is. I suspect a few get caught and a lot get burnt.

This image of *kupisa uswa* came to me when *The Herald* reported the Kenyan police reaction to the Mungiki sect. Seemingly this sect is notorious for terrorising people and killing them in gruesome ways. Kenyans want the sect crushed but they are horrified with the way the authorities try to do it. One thousand heavily armed police descended on their suspected hide-out of the sect in the Mathare slums of Nairobi and killed 34 people. It appears little effort was made to sort out who was guilty and who was innocent. Families were seen fleeing the 'police terror' and residents interviewed expressed deep hatred for the police. 'There was no proper investigation, no intelligence was used,' they said.

It is painstaking and often frustrating work to diagnose an illness and to investigate a crime in society. It is easier to simply blunder in with overwhelming force. This is what the American government did when they 'conquered' Iraq with no understanding or plan about what would happen next. Now those in favour of removing Sadam Hussein by force and starting a war in the process are surprised to find themselves hated rather than thanked. The country has become a battleground between

Shiites and Sunnis.[1] Minorities, like the Jews and Christians who have lived in Iraq unmolested for two millennia, are being driven out. And huge numbers of Iraqi Muslims are fleeing their own country to seek refuge in Jordan and Syria.

But let us bring the image home to our land. The heavy hand of force has been in use many times – by the Rhodesians in their long colonial occupation and in their 'war against terror' and later by our present government in Matabeleland, on the commercial farms, the informal homes and businesses and now in the high-density suburbs. Police are now roaming the streets, indiscriminately terrorising anyone about late at night.

When the heavy hand of indiscriminate force is used the conclusion must be that the government wants to instill fear generally among the people so that once more it may 'conquer' when the time comes for elections. But burning the grass destroys everything and may yield no results. It leaves the country scarred and vulnerable to erosion.

13 June, 2007

---

1 Two Islamic sects with different beliefs, particularly with regard to who should have succeeded the first great Islamic prophet Mohamed.

29

WE HAD HOPED

I saw a man at a traffic light selling solar panels. At least I thought that was what he was doing, I thought, 'great! a man has devised a way of beating the cuts and shortages. He has invented a portable solar power unit.' My hopes rose. Even the poorest in the rural areas might afford something so small. In a fraction of a second I saw the solution to the country's energy woes.

But then reality struck. As I drew nearer, I saw he was holding up toilet rolls. We long for sparks of hope but sparks are ephemeral. They seldom catch fire. Still, we scan the media for the signs behind the headlines. Lately, word spread that we might join the rand area. In a stroke, one of our biggest problems would be solved. We would be tied to a stable currency. The very next day that hope was dashed. And so it continues.

In the Gospel of Luke (Chap. 24) two people are joined by a companion as they walk to the village of Emmaus. One of them, Cleophas, speaks of his broken dreams. He lamented the one just executed in Jerusalem. 'We had hoped that he would be the one to set [us] free.' We followed him and spent hours listening to him. We really thought he would do something for us. What Cleophas didn't realise was that it was Jesus himself who was their new companion and he had come precisely to show them what real hope was. It was not just vague allegiance to an idea or indeed a person who is good at making promises. It involves an engagement, a way of life and values. 'How is it you don't understand,' Jesus chided the two, 'that the Messiah had to suffer and so enter his glory?'

'Had to suffer'? Do Zimbabweans *have to* suffer? No! Or at least not in the way they are doing. But real meaningful 'hope' is a tough concept. It is not a fleeting wish that costs little. It is a commitment to the truth come what may. It is founded on an assurance that no matter what falsity and perversity surrounds us, the truth will prevail and herald a new world.

We are paying for our passivity these past twenty years and more. If we hope for a new Zimbabwe it is time to be engaged in achieving it. Otherwise we will continue like the people in the fuel queue for three days and nights and end up laughing; 'this [the country we are now used to] is the Zimbabwe we want'.

30 July, 2007

30

WHY IS ALL THIS HAPPENING TO US?

In the midst of Midianite oppression, Gideon, not Gono (Governor of the Reserve Bank) but the other one, was threshing wheat (Judges 6:11) when the angel of the Lord appeared to him and said, 'the Lord is with you'. Gideon replies, 'if the Lord is with us why is all this [hardship] happening to us?' Good question! It has been asked constantly ever since. We ask it in Zimbabwe today. Why do the wicked prosper?

In Psalm 73 the psalmist is perplexed by their prosperity: 'For them no such thing as pain / their bodies are healthy and strong / they do not suffer as other men do / .../ pride is their chain of honour / violence the garment that covers them / their spite oozes like fat / their hearts drip with slyness... / they think their mouth is heaven / and their tongue can dictate on earth.' A little later he says, 'I tried to analyse the problem, hard though I found it / until the day I pierced the mystery / and saw the end in store for them /...'

God cannot do anything about evil. Once he created the world and all the people in it, he bound himself to the choices people make. A Jewish Rabbi was once asked the question, 'where was God in Auschwitz?'[1] He replied, 'He was there in the camp with the people who were being

---

1 A network of camps where 1.1 million Jews, as well a several hundred Romanies and Jehova Witness were ruthlessly exterminated like vermin during the Second World War.

killed.' He walked with them to the gas chambers.

So what is the point of prayer if God is not going to do something?' God does not interfere in human decisions. Because God loves us, God respects our choices as any loving parent does the foibles of their teenage son or daughter. The point of prayer is that it open us up to God so that we can hear his voice, recognise his nudging and look honestly at our choices. It is we who change and in our changing we bring about what we long for. We do not understand all this but we know that God can enter a person's life at any time and draw them to a new path. Thomas Aquinas wrote eight hundred years ago something like this, 'God does not cause evil, neither does he want it. But he permits it and that is good.' It is possible to glimpse somehow that blocking people from acting – even if they do something stupid, bad or really evil – takes away from their freedom. It is through facing evil, struggling against it in ourselves and in the world, that we grow to maturity. Jesus came precisely to help us to do this. He accompanied us all the way, even to Golgotha. So, Gideon, there is some kind of answer for you.

21 August, 2007

31

HOW LONG?

How long, Lord, am I to cry for help
While you will not listen;
To cry 'Oppression' in your ear
And you will not save?

Habakkuk voices a mood that people have often felt in human history and we feel today in Zimbabwe. Why do we go on suffering year after year without any intervention from our God who loves us?

I met strong dissent two days ago when I suggested that Ian Smith has some responsibility for the present situation. 'It has nothing to do with Smith,' I was told, 'it is all the responsibility of the present government'. Certainly the government could act far more wisely and compassionately than they are doing but we cannot escape the history that formed us for good or ill. Smith himself flourished for a time because he rode on the crest of a wave of feeling that had been growing among his constituents for decades. He played on the fears of the minority who were the ones at that time who had the vote. The long history of segregation from the late twenties and early thirties bred a fertile seed-bed for the Rhodesian Front. The settlers who made the early decisions to turn their back on working with the sons and daughters of the soil – and exclude them from a meaningful partnership – are the ones who set the trend. Smith was the logical heir of such decisions.

Blaming Smith now is a fairly fruitless exercise but assigning him some responsibility helps to understand the present. Because he was such a particularly intransigent expression of the trend set long before, he was very hard to remove. In the end the people of the land decided they could only win freedom by force. But here again there were heirs and our present leader is the principal one. Intransigence can only be removed by force, he concluded, but in the process he learnt all the ways of intransigence – and force.

So we are back where we were thirty years ago and again our leaders aren't listening to the people. The difference this time is that no one wants to remove them by force. We want to do it peacefully as they did recently in Sierra Leone where an unpopular government was simply voted out of office. Yet is will not be that easy. The old habits, learnt from Smith – foremost among them, intransigence – persist.

So what does Habakkuk have to say? A little further he has this, 'the upright person will love by his faithfulness'. Faithfulness! What is that? It is a quality of attention and patience that looks for solutions everywhere but does not lose hope when there seems to be none immediately in sight.

3 October, 2007

32

DON'T MAKE US LAUGH

Less than a year before he became the first American President to resign, Richard Nixon made a speech in which he insisted, 'I am not a crook.' He subsequently proved to be one. In the course of his presidency Bill Clinton had occasion to assert, 'I did not have sex with that woman.' It subsequently came out that he did. So when Gideon Gono, Reserve Bank Governor, comes out with his remark that we, in the Reserve Bank, 'are not buffoons,' one might be excused for holding one's breath.

I visited a restaurant recently where every table was taken in the middle of the week and everyone there was white. I recognised just one person and asked the owners who all these people were. They did not look like NGO blow-ins or diplomats. He assured me there were all local long-term residents and began to describe the tables. Those people at the far end have been in the country for forty years, that other table for twenty. So what are they all doing here on a Wednesday night spending three times a teacher's monthly salary on a bottle of South African wine? The answer was straightforward. 'They have no food at home so they come here to eat.'

Why begrudge those who can afford it if they choose to find their food in restaurants? But what of those, like a man I met today, who earns a salary as a guard of three and a half million dollars (more than a teacher) and cannot afford food – to say nothing of rent and school fees for his five children? We keep wondering how people manage? The simple answer is, 'they don't.' We are a country of malnourished people yet we know we have the capacity to feed ourselves and half of Southern Africa. The thesaurus describes a buffoon as a clown, a comedian or a joker. All three professions make us laugh and since we do a lot of that one might be excused for thinking that, like Nixon and Clinton, Gono is just what he says he is not. Every time a new nail is driven into our economic coffin our first reaction is to laugh.

The gulf between rich and poor grows wider each day. It is becoming unbearable. Soon people will be too hungry and exhausted even to laugh.

24 October, 2007

33

SHIPWRECK

As a landlocked country we can't perhaps easily imagine what a shipwreck must be like. But it must be terrifying as you realise the forces of nature against you are so overwhelming and there is little you can do to save yourself. The coast around the South African Cape has seen an estimated 1,000 such wrecks in the last 500 years. Among all of these, one stands out.

It was some time in the eighteenth century and the 'Cape of Storms' was living up to its name. A ship, I forget the details, was at anchor but with the force of the gale it dragged its anchor and found itself on the rocks some distance from the shore. The company that owned the ship were more interested in saving their cargo than saving the sailors who were left to their own devices. A few managed to swim to safety but others drowned in the attempt. The remainder clung to the wreck and hoped for the best.

It happened that a man rode down on his horse to bring lunch to his son, who was working by the sea. Seeing the desperation of the wrecked sailors he goaded his horse into the stormy waters and swam out to the wreck. When he reached it he told two of the sailors to cling to the horse's tail and he then towed them to land. He did this seven times and so rescued fourteen sailors. By this time both he and his horse were exhausted. His son pleaded with him not to go again but the cries of the remaining sailors were unbearable to him and once more man and horse plunged into the sea. The stranded sailors realised that this would be their last chance so they all jumped into the sea and clung to the horse. In doing so they pulled the animal under the waves and all including the horse were drowned.

It is a sad story but an inspiring one of someone who did not count the cost to himself in trying to save others. It strikes me this tale is a mirror in which we can look at ourselves. We will see different things but what clearly stands out is the age old concern for wealth over people, for capital rather than labour, concern for profits rather than for the vulnerable. The company that owned the ship actually set up a gallows to hang instantly anyone who approached the salvaged cargo.

But then also there is that lamentable human gut response, seen in that last act where everyone just thinks of him or herself and pulls the whole state, as it were, under the waves, destroying good men in the process. In a desperate bid to get what I want, I destroy the lives of others.

11 January, 2008

34

HELL

For people today hell is a hard idea to grasp. In former ages people accepted the idea of hell and it entered into literature and painting without question. But in our time we find it hard, no matter how evil a person has been in his or her life, to imagine them in hell for eternity.

Yet hell is simply an extension in one direction of the great gift of God, which is human life and human freedom. If he gives us these gifts it means we have to accept the consequences of them. If we make good choices we are enriching the lives of everyone around us and ensuring that we too will enjoy life here and hereafter. When I say 'enjoy', I do not mean that life will always be pleasant. It may be filled with struggles and challenges. But at a deep level there will be a happiness that no one can take away. When Pedro Arrupe, a former general superior of the Jesuits, emerged from a month of solitary confinement in a Japanese jail (he was falsely accused of spying for the Americans) he astonished his guards by thanking them. Despite his sufferings in an unheated jail in winter with unpalatable food he was deeply happy during that month. He made it a retreat in solidarity with the sufferings of Jesus in his people everywhere. Such people make a choice to live their lives to the full in accordance with the simple prayer, 'thy will be done'. By doing so they inevitably reach heaven or whatever you want to call the life 'God has prepared for those who love him' (1 Cor 2:9).

If, on the other hand, we make bad choices and get into the habit of trampling on our conscience and become increasingly accustomed to wrong-doing, well, then we have freely chosen hell. We have made ourselves evil people and it is almost impossible to change such people. Really hardened drug criminals, torturers and exploiters of others in all sorts of ways chose to be that way. They simply shut out any suggestion that they should do otherwise. Today we find this whole concept of someone being so evil that there is not even a spark of goodness somewhere in him or her deeply uncomfortable. As I say, earlier generations had no problem with this possibility.

Jesus confirmed the Jewish tradition as found, for example, in the last words of Isaiah (66:24, see Mark 9:48),

> *Their worm will never die*
> *nor their fire be put out*

We do not get a description of hell in the Bible beyond such imagery as this, but this is enough. The worm that will not die can be seen as the habit that will not change. If people make evil decisions that little by little become hardened habits, they simply create their own hell. After death their decision is confirmed by the reality that awaits them.

20 January, 2008

35

DRIP FEEDING THE RESULTS

Turning into College Road by the university this morning I noticed a new bill board: SPEED DOESN'T LEAD TO PROGRESS. IT'S DIRECTION THAT COUNTS. During this past month we have had neither speed nor direction. The final results of the election are now out, but is there any confidence that we have an idea where we are going? There is evidence of violence in selected areas and many have fled their homes. There are documented reports of torture and death. What are we doing to ourselves?

One commentator, in the early days after the elections, spoke of 'drip feeding the results'. A patient who is ill is drip fed because he cannot take solid food. It is now five weeks since Election Day and we have only just been given the official figures. All the explanations for the delay sound hollow. Where in the world does it take five weeks to count votes – especially where there are relatively few voters and communications are reasonably good?

It was a crime, during the Smith era, to say or do anything that would 'cause alarm or despondency' as the Rhodesians set about bolstering their unreal world. Surely the practice lingers? Perhaps releasing the results as they were counted would have caused alarm and despondency? But to whom? To continue the medical analogy: we have to admit that this whole sad saga means we are not a healthy society.

But we don't admit it. Crisis? What crisis? Some of the people, those who have power and wealth, want things to go on as they are. They are in denial. Everything is okay. But for most people, life is one long, almost unbearable, endurance test with no end in sight. Every day they have to look for food and all the other basic necessities of life. The government has not addressed these issues. No practical steps have been taken to ease the suffering of the people. The opposite seems to be true. We now join many countries in the world in having IDPs (internally displaced persons) – a very real symptom of a sick society.

The night is darkest just before dawn. We are about to end the season of Easter with celebration of Pentecost. It was an event that gave life and meaning to everything that had gone before. And it wasn't just an obscure event in a remote corner of a small country all those years ago. It's meaning lives with us now.

3 May, 2008

36

RESPECTING THE PEOPLE

I am not sure how many of us even noticed it but last week it was big news in Europe: the Irish voted 'no' to the Lisbon Treaty. It was a proposal to streamline decision making in a community of 27 nations but the Irish thought it was giving too much power to unelected bureaucrats in Brussels, the administrative hub of the European Union. There was consternation in Berlin, Paris, London and the other capital cities but there was also a realisation that this vote – by one percent of the population of Europe - had to be respected because that was the agreement: if even one country of the 27 rejected the treaty it would have to be scrapped.

It was notable that whatever their views on a united Europe, people had nothing to say about the actual vote. It was received with respect because it was the people themselves speaking. Whether you agree with them or not is beside the point: this is what they want. 'All you need to say is "yes" if you mean yes, "no" if you mean no; anything more than this comes from the Evil One' (Matthew 5:37).

In Zimbabwe, we are desperately trying to say 'No' but who is listening? We are trying to say no to wild inflation, shortage of food, lack of medicine, the collapse of schools, corruption and the general breakdown of the state. We now have a chance to actually speak our 'no' – or our 'yes' if we are so inclined – but this opportunity is being deliberately taken away from us in a most violent fashion.

People have endured so much already but now they are being asked to endure even more, and for an unknown period. The only thing we can be certain of is that eventually the people of violence only win relatively short-term victories. They are then shunted aside, and their names are regarded with abhorrence by succeeding generations.

16 June, 2008

37

THE POINT OF NO RETURN

The Cuban missile crisis of 1962 must rank as the closest human beings have come to nuclear war and therefore the biggest military catastrophe ever. But we were saved by the wisdom of one man. President Kennedy had read *The Guns of August*[1] about the outbreak of the First World War, the greatest cataclysm till then, and was determined that future generations would not repeat the question asked by the soldiers giving their lives in the trenches, 'why are we fighting?' So when the Cuban crisis came he, alone among his advisers, cautioned restraint. He enabled both sides to withdraw with dignity.

It takes wisdom and self-control to practice restraint. Today, in our country, all restraint seems to have vanished. Young people are forced to torture other young people – and not so young people – without any regard for what this is doing to their own lives, to the lives of their victims and to the country as a whole. The media of the world is describing day after day what is happening in Zimbabwe and our leaders just don't care. They seem to have reached a point when they think they are untouchable. Let the world go hang. No justice will ever catch up with me. The psalmist writes, 'the fool says in his heart, "there is no God"'.

At first a little corruption, a few lies and a bit of violence are

---

1 *The Guns of August* by Barbara W. Tuchman: Penguin Random House, New York 1962. A Pulitzer prize-winning book about the earliest stages of the First World War.

hardly noticed. They may touch my conscience a little but I soon brush them aside. But then there are pressures from others (my leaders, for example) or self-interest that pushes me to go on doing these things. I become used to them until finally I have reached a point where there is no going back. There is no return. I have stamped on my conscience until it is dead.

People have used the word 'war' in Zimbabwe recently and it started by just being a political threat; heavy language to pressure people into submission. I suppose like most people I have brushed aside the thought that we really could be returning to war: that brother would set about killing brother and sister killing sister. I have read accounts of Rwanda in 1994 and said that could never happen here.

But the events of the last five weeks have made me shudder. Is civil strife now going to escalate to such an extent that no one can control it? Can our leaders not see the way we are going? If we continue as we are no one will be a winner. And our children and grandchildren will ask 'why did they do it?' What were they fighting about? Please, it is time for wiser counsel. It is time to stop the violence. Soon it will be too late. We will have reached the point of no return. Violence so often breeds violence.

5 July, 2008

38

A GREAT WEARINESS

Everywhere there is great weariness. Everyone you meet has his or her tale of struggle. The great sickness continues and it needs constant nutritious food to fight it. But how do we find this food? Some are not sick but in tears: They cannot find food to feed their children. Crowds wait patiently by the roadside for someone to stop. When you do stop you will hear more tales of woe. When you go to the schools you will see many of them closed and the children idle. When you go to the prison you hear of deaths from starvation. Then there is the violence, constant violence against people, including the violence of preventing food from reaching those in need. And there is the lack of money and the high prices and the shortage of goods. All of this is compounded by a resolve not to do anything about it by those who could do something.

Many countries in recent months have faced disasters from droughts, floods and cyclones. Thousands have been made homeless and many have died but the countries concerned work all out to help the victims and bring relief. Why are we not doing the same? Why are we actually going the other way and preventing those who want to help from doing so? History will scrutinise our time and condemn us for our coldness of heart.

Even this list is wearisome. It has been drawn up so many times before. And it goes on and on.

Some countries have shown neglect, incompetence, discrimination and they have used dictatorial methods. But was there ever a country that actually set out to frustrate initiatives in financial management, efforts in informal employment, measures that would advance accountability and the free flow of information?

As I write, people are going to bed hungry all over the land. Tomorrow they will start all over again searching for ways of simply surviving.

And there is no good bringing religion in to soften the pain, to provide a tranquillizer. God will not do, cannot do, a single thing to help us until we move ourselves. There is no good praying on a Sunday and doing despicable things on a Monday. We would be better off listening to Habakkuk:

> *The fig does not blossom*
> *nor fruit grow on the vine.*
> *The olive crop fails*
> *and the fields produce no harvest*
> *The flocks vanish from the folds*
> *and the stalls stand empty of cattle.*
> *Even so I will rejoice in the Lord*
> *and exult in God my Saviour*

7 September, 2008

39

MISSING THE POINT

The country is dry, barren and burnt. We say we love our country, and have a spiritual association with it, and we allow it to burn, destroying trees, small animals, birds and insects in the process; careless of our power and our cruelty.

But in the midst of this desolation, sometimes you can suddenly see a *mutamba*, dazzling green, defying the sun and the surrounding man-made desert. Nature can still lift our hearts, especially at this time of the year. Flowers and shrubs insist on being noticed – purples and reds and yellows – all reminding us that recovery can happen. It is a miracle but not one on which we should rely.

Does this describe our mood? The power-sharing agreement between ZANU-PF and the MDC has lain on the table for weeks and there seems no apparent urgency to put flesh to it. Rumours swirl around raising dust like the whirlwinds of this season.

I have been reading Paul's first letter to the Corinthians and his central point is forever relevant. He had struggled to found a little community in this sophisticated busy and prosperous trading city. He thought it was well established and he could move on to other places but he gets reports that there are dissensions among them. As soon as his back was turned they started vying for positions. There were different groups – some for Apollo, some for Paul, some for Cephas – and the question seems to have been which one would come out on top. They lost sight of the whole point of their community, which was to nourish the faith of the believers and help them live the new life and gradually transform the society in which they lived. You can feel Paul's anger as he writes, 'Has Christ been parceled out? Was it Paul that was crucified for you?' (Cor 1:13).

We easily lose sight of the vision. We miss the point. If the rumours are even half true they are shameful; it seems people are far more interested in who gets what position than in getting the country out of the ditch. People are starving. There are reports that people are actually dying in our prisons for want of food. Do we ever think of the harsh judgment our grandchildren will pass on us? 'They could have easily done something but they put their private interests before the common good.' It will not be a pretty verdict.

But maybe, just maybe, this coming week someone will engage with the spirit of renewal, someone will put the country first not themselves?

28 September, 2008

40

A HOUSE IN RUINS

August, 520 BC. The prophet Haggai chides the people returning from the exile for building their own houses first and neglecting the building of the temple. 'Is this a time for you to live in your paneled houses when this House lies in ruins?' It seems a severe judgment. Surely they should settle themselves first before embarking on some bigger project? But I don't think that is Haggai's point. He is hinting at priorities. Everyone is busy sorting out their own affairs while the larger affairs of the community, the nation, are neglected. We don't have to reflect much to realise that this is always the way we are tempted to act.

The culture that we have created for ourselves in Zimbabwe is one where everyone is thinking of themselves and their survival. And who can blame them? Conditions are so tough that it has become a full-time occupation. I needn't list the daily occupations of walking to town, queuing at banks, searching for food and so forth. But the problem is that it overflows into dishonest short-cuts; helping oneself from others' groceries, holding back ten litres of fuel for me when pouring fifty for you, using this and that opportunity to get something for myself. And when I start on this road of cheating you, my conscience alerts me at first. But if I persist I will soon quiet my conscience. Cheating and twisting the truth becomes habitual. A nation can lose its integrity. That, it seems, is what lies behind Haggai's warning.

Several papers have carried a photo of the signing of the 'power sharing agreement' in which the President is seen really happy and smiling at his opponent whose face is only partly visible. The smile seems unbelievable in the light of what has happened these past four weeks. What was he so happy about? That they had worked out a good deal that would benefit the people? If so why do we still not have a working government a month after the signing? Or was he happy because he had neutralised his challenger by absorbing him on to his own side? As the days and weeks go by this has to be a likely conclusion. Meanwhile the 'temple', the bigger project of rebuilding the country, lies in ruins.

12 October, 2008

41

POWER

I met a man last week who had never been to Africa but blew in for three days and told me there would be a settlement this week. I hope he is right as we have been waiting for 43 years (since UDI) and more for a 'settlement.' Independence seemed like one for a time but it did not provide a lasting accord which satisfied everyone. These past weeks we have heightened expectations of a settlement but so far it eludes us. Perhaps between the writing of these words and their appearance in print we will have one?

But what makes one doubt is the way people abuse the power they have. Imagine agreeing to meet someone and then denying them the means to come to the meeting? Too often power is exercised as though it has no implications. I display my power and I do not care about the consequences. But there are always consequences. The settlers in this country made a deliberate choice a hundred years ago to use power to preserve and develop their hold on the country and its resources. When the local people started to enter the economy in the 1920s the settlers deliberately devised legislation to limit their access to land, industry and education. Over the years more and tighter legislation was introduced to bolster this policy. By the 1970s it led to violence and war.

And the habit of violence became embedded in the land so that even after independence in remained with us and is still with us. Oh yes, there are consequences.

The true use of power is when a person uses it to bring about what people are longing for. Think of South Africa. Naked power was used to divide people for decades, even centuries. But in the last quarter of the last century a slow painful movement gradually became unstoppable to bring about a settlement that everybody, but a few extremists, wanted. This was the use of power to bring about something that inherently was right and so it will last. Think of Europe. Hitler conquered it with military might in a few years and tried to hold it by force. He failed. Then the Europeans set out to unite it themselves over a period of 60 years, slowly and painfully building a consensus, and they are succeeding. Why? Because they are using their power to achieve something that is inherently what people want – peace and stability.

When we read the letters of Paul we see him constantly talking about power. Take, for example, the one to the Ephesians (3:16ff), 'May He through his Spirit, enable you to grow firm in power with regard to your inner self so that Christ may live in your hearts through faith ...' What power is he talking about? He is pointing to the inner ability to work for what is really the right thing to do in any situation. It takes power, the right use of power, to do what is right to resolve our problems and begin to feed our people. That is the inner strength we need. All this pandering to external power that gives me some momentary advantage but has no lasting effect for good is just selfish and ephemeral.

26 October, 2008

42

A FAILURE OF IMAGINATION

I hope the leader of the largest party in Parliament, the one who won the most votes (as agreed by everyone – friend and foe alike) in the first round of the elections, knows that his steadiness in the present impasse is inspiring. He is standing his ground and, though for a short time more the pain will be prolonged, he is laying a sure foundation for the politics of the future. We live through a civil contest, not of guns but of words, between people of conviction and people of fear.

The Irish writer, John Banville, was asked a few years ago why he had not written about the 30-year struggle in Northern Ireland between those who wanted civil freedoms and those who wanted to preserve their privileged way of life. He responded by talking about a novel he had written, *The Book of Evidence*, which while not mentioning Ireland was about 'failure to imagine other people into existence' – a state of mind which allowed people to 'plant a bomb in a crowded street' because 'the people walking around in the street are not really human.'

In the actual book there is a scene where Freddie kills a girl who came across him in the act of stealing a valuable work of art. In his prison cell he ponders about what he has done. He cannot say he did not mean to kill her but he cannot tell when he really began to mean to do it. For him she did not really exist:

> *'[W]hen she crouched in the car and I hit her again and
> again and her blood spattered the window. This is the*

> worst, the essential sin, I think, the one for which there
> will be no forgiveness: that I never imagined her vividly
> enough, that I never made her be there sufficiently, that
> I did not make her live. Yes, that failure of imagination
> is my real crime, the one that made the others possible.
> What I told that policeman is true – I killed her because I
> could kill her, and I could kill her because for me she was
> not alive.'

The decisions that are made – or avoided – in the late night /
early morning meetings where our future is discussed are a result
of a 'failure of imagination'. The people whose future depends on
these discussions do not really exist for some of the participants
in these gatherings. And so for them it is a small step to reach
the point where they fail to imagine the suffering and death they
are causing by their avoidance of deciding to act. Barack Obama,
in his victory speech after being elected as the first African-
American President of the United States, spoke of one old black
lady of 106 who had lived through a century of oppression and
dawning freedom to see the day when a black man was elected
the President of the US. He had the imagination to think of her.
Could our leaders imagine one – just one – of our 'born free'
children, feet bare, clothes patched, searching for roots and wild
fruits in the dry land when he or she should be at school?

12 November, 2008.

43

DILEMMA

We have been reflecting on it all week. Basildon Peta set the tone in his forceful commentary after waiting up till 3.00 a.m. to attend every press conference given by the participants: they just didn't have the courage (he used more earthy language) to stand up to him (Mugabe). A colleague expressed it this way: under pressure, the dominant value that people act out of is not justice and concern for the common good. Rather it is the desire to maintain harmony amongst peers, whatever the cost. In other words, what really matters is not the people out there but the people in here.

> *The creepered wall stands up to hide*
> *The gathering multitude outside*
> *Whose glances hunger worsens;*
> *Concealing from their wretchedness*
> *Our metaphysical distress*
> *Our kindness to ten persons.*

W. H. Auden here points to the uncomfortable dilemma we can experience when we know what we ought to do but we just cannot summon up the courage to do it. Among public servants we look for courage and integrity but we do not find it. And because in our situation those who are in positions to act do not do so, the long betrayal continues.

A woman was widowed recently and her late husband's brother

wanted to 'inherit' her as a wife. She refused. He then took over one of her fields and built a house there. She contested this in court and won the case. He then threatened to burn her house down and even hinted that he could kill her.

This woman followed the law and acted freely and bravely. But in the circumstances she risked destroying relationships within her family and ruining her own life by not giving in to the overwhelming weight of custom and tradition. In other words, she was faced with an impossible choice: either to give in to her husband's brother and lose her happiness, or make her stand and maybe lose her life.

Our politicians may feel they are faced with impossible choices. In both the private and the public realm we seem to be unable to peg out the dimensions of courage: its cost and its benefits. Possibly the former are now too great. To act on principle is to surrender the many benefits of working for a regime which uses carrot and stick. So we run away from decisions that are painful. And thus the moral climate that we have created over the past eight years is not conducive to truth, principle, honour or justice.

It is some consolation to know that Paul was aware of the dilemma: 'for though the will to do what is good is in me, the performance is not, with the result that instead of doing the good things I want to do, I carry out the sinful things I do not want' (Romans 7:18-19). But Paul pointed the way to the remedy.

14 November, 2008

44

EROSION

Erosion rarely happens overnight. The well-trodden path gradually gives way to a small gully. And the next time you pass that way the gully has become a gorge.

Two pictures have haunted me this week. The first is of a woman lying in a Harare street with her child playing close by. A frequent sight? Yes, but this time the woman is dead. And her child doesn't know it and continues to play. People begin to realise and gather and stare. And the child doesn't understand. Eventually a woman covers the body with a *chitenge*. What happens to the child we wonder?

The second picture is of an uncle rushing his child to the hospital. The boy took poison to end his painful life. The uncle is desperate and asks the nurses to help but they are on strike and refuse. 'At least tell me what to do to save him,' he pleads. But they refuse again and the child dies in his arms.

These are just two recent events. What if all our stories are told? The erosion of our society has become a huge *goronga*. I met a woman who told me 50 people are dying of cholera every day in Budiriro. Allowing for exaggeration, she is still saying they are many.

Mark tells us of some words of Jesus about 'the land producing first the shoot, then the ear, then the full grain in the ear ... and then the crop is ready' (4:28). Unfortunately he also spoke of weeds among the wheat (Matthew 13:25), which would also grow in the same way.

How do you cure erosion? If you act early enough you can prevent it. But if you let it go on and on you are left with a mighty wound, a huge scar, such as is plainly visible (even from satellites in space, no doubt) in Mhondoro.

How will we ever heal the wounds in our society? They are so deep. Corruption, like violence, has become so embedded in our way of doing things. It is as contagious as cholera.

It is said that people do not die of starvation where there is a free press. It is easy to see why this is true. Once you publicise a situation you are half way to a remedy. But we are in denial about so much. Meanwhile the erosion continues.

22 November, 2008

45

LOSING OUR SOUL

In 1941 Irène Némirowsky sat down to write a book about the fall of France and the effects of the German occupation. She never completed the work as she was sent to the extermination camp in Auschwitz the following year. Her daughter, a school girl at the time and herself hunted by the police so that she should share the fate of her mother, kept the manuscript but could not bear to look at it for over 60 years. Finally, 65 years after Némirowsky's death the book appeared and caused a sensation. This is how she wrote:

> *The people around him, his family, his friends, aroused a feeling of shame and rage within him. He had seen them on the road, them and people like them; he recalled the cars full of officers running away with their beautiful yellow trunks and their painted women, civil servants abandoning their posts, panic-stricken politicians dropping files of secret papers along the road, young girls, who had diligently wept the day the armistice was signed, being comforted in the arms of the Germans. 'And to think that no one will know, that there will be such a conspiracy of lies that all this will be transformed into yet another glorious page in the history of France. We'll do everything we can to find acts of devotion and heroism of the official records. Good God! To see what I've seen. Closed doors where you knock in vain to get a glass of water and*

> *refugees who pillage houses; everywhere, everywhere*
> *you look, chaos, cowardice, vanity and ignorance! What a*
> *wonderful race we are!'*

I ventured into SPAR in Mount Pleasant a few days before Christmas and there was total gridlock as trolleys overflowing with provisions waited their turn to pay their US dollars. Earlier in the day I had met some people who were beside themselves with anger at being unable to access their own money in the bank and once again my stomach churned as I experienced the 'two nations' – those who have managed to find a way of living comfortably in a crisis situation and the many who are defeated, frustrated and angry.

We are not an 'occupied' country as France was in the early 1940s, except in the sense that there is a palpable sense of 'them' and 'us.' But we are a defeated one, defeated by our own government, driven like the defeated everywhere to flee, to hunt, to cheat and to push the weak aside. What is crushingly painful is that we are in danger of losing our soul. People are pushing others aside, or simply writing them out, in a way we have never done before. Hatred, bitterness and cruelty are seeping into our being. As we approach a New Year it will become ever more urgent that we fight this drift to despair. One day we will need to learn compassion and forgiveness again. We really have to begin to prepare for that day.

22 December, 2008

46

DIVIDED MINDS AND HEARTS

It was only 7.00 on a May morning and the two were already sweating. One was stripped to the waist. They were pushing a wheelbarrow and a hand-cart both filled with firewood for sale at the cement factory residences. They had already covered twelve of the fourteen kilometers from forests near Arcturus. 'What can we do? There is hunger. We have to live.'

On 1 May there was a report that the International Monetary Fund estimates it will cost US\$45 billion just to get Zimbabwe to where it was in 1995. We have lived through fourteen years of deterioration and ruin of the economy and it has reduced people to pushing wheelbarrows loaded with logs fourteen kms in the middle of the night just to stay alive.

If we could just set about the reconstruction with everyone united and pulling together our spirits would rise. But we cannot do that because those who make the decisions and operate the levers of power are pulling against each other. There are those among them who always have two thoughts where they should only have one. They have divided minds. They think of the job to be done and they think at the same time of how the doing of it will effect their own position. If doing the job will reflect badly on them then they don't do it.

This must be obvious even to the begrudgers and obstructers themselves. But they do it anyway. Grudges are as old as history. Wasn't Abel the victim of a grudge?

So the 'cautious optimism' of the early days of the shared government is fast ebbing away. It is proving so difficult to get anything done. Those who do not give up and keep trying are like those early morning handcart pushers. They are lighting a lamp rather than cursing the darkness. The darkness is all around us. Yet if the number of those who light lamps steadily increases a new dawn will come.

And I don't buy into the 'where we were in 1995' sound bite. Economically and socially we may be far from what we were then and, to be fair, that is all that is meant. But we have gained much wisdom since. People are much more aware of what has happened, what is happening and what should happen then they ever were then. Frankly, we were half asleep at that time. We should never have had to go through such suffering to wake us up. But at the end of the day we are awake. And if they haven't already, our politicians will soon discover it.

8 May, 2009

47

A GOVERNMENT OF CLOSED DOORS

ZANU-PF is stuck like a car on clay after a heavy downpour. All they can do is rev the engine giving them a sense of doing something. But they are going nowhere. Meanwhile their passengers are held up and cannot reach their destination. Whether we like it or not they are in the driving seat.

Jean Vanier is an eighty-year-old Canadian who has devoted his life to welcoming people with intellectual disabilities into homes where they can live as normal a life as possible and develop their gifts. As a young man he was appalled to see such people trapped in institutions where they simply existed. They had no proper life. He recognised their unspoken cry of pain, their longing for relationship and a sense of worth. In 1964 he opened his first house in France and welcomed two people, Raphael and Philippe, who had been locked up for years in an institution.

He thought he was doing something good for them and he cooked (not very well by his own admission) and cared for them. But gradually he realised that he had opened a door to something amazing. Raphael and Philippe did not just want care. They wanted friendship and the opportunity to exercise their gifts. To meet their demands Jean had to slow down, learn their 'language', try to enter into their pain, and gradually build up the sort of relationship that would give them the courage to open up. He did this and a whole movement (l'Arche (the Ark) of Noah – a place of refuge and hope) was born. There are now around 140 l'Arche communities all over the world, including Zimbabwe.

On Easter Sunday Jean was interviewed on the radio and he reflected on the implications of this opening up to people who are different. He quoted the gospel where Jesus says, when you are having a meal, don't invite your relatives and friends because they will just invite you back. If you are having a meal, a celebration, invite the poor, the lame, the outcasts, the handicapped – and you will be blessed (Luke 14:12-14). What kind of blessing is this? It is the blessing of receiving after you have taken the first step of welcoming the one who is different.

So much in our society, in our politics, revolves around interacting with those who think like us. Remember the early 1980s. Black and white were now working in the same offices, the same work places and got on quite well during the day. But come evening the whites went their way and the blacks theirs. The breaking down of barriers was superficial. We did not really open our doors to those who were different. And the tendency escalated when the whites became marginalised. Then blacks started to close their doors on each other and so it is today. And we have a government of closed doors.

25 May, 2009

48

ONE PEOPLE, ONE NATION – NOT YET

Sometime in the 1930s King George V remarked, 'we are all middle class now.' Maybe he spoke tongue in cheek but he was referring to the levelling off in society brought about by democracy. People could no longer see to their own advantage without regard for others. It was not so long before that society in the UK had been divided. I came across this story of life in Ireland (while it was still part of the UK) in the nineteenth century:

> *Ikey liked to be called a Tinker as it seemed to him to best describe his culture. He remembered being told how the English landlords who owned most of the land got them evicted, and put them out on the roadside and their little thatched cottages were burnt to the ground. Trying to keep body, soul and family together they quickly learnt the craft of the tinsmith. They travelled the country making buckets, pots and pans and showing great skills in repairing milk churns and other farm and kitchen utensils. These were honest people who worked their way around the country, never looking for charity and always willing to work to keep the wolf from the door.*

Such injustice would be inconceivable in the England or Ireland of today because the rulers are on their toes to pay attention to every whim and opinion of the voters. There is fury in the UK at the moment about the 'allowances' the MPs have been giving themselves and heads will roll at the next election.

Yet in our own land we are nowhere near such sensibility. Murambatsvina did to people what the English landlords did but no one has been held accountable. Painfully we have patched together an 'inclusive agreement' but it is not working very well. Those with power to act, lack the will, and those with the will, lack the power. Meanwhile, with unemployment over 90% the people just watch. For some there has been some small improvement. For most there is just more and more suffering. The scriptures spoke long ago of participation, a sharing, communion in the covenant established by the Lord, which would create one people. The blood poured by Moses over the altar and the people was a symbol of the unity that would be fully effected in the shedding of the blood of Jesus; in his giving of himself for all people on Calvary. It would draw them into unity. That is still the goal, however much we continue to resist it and refuse to live as brother and sister.

13 June, 2009

2

DISCOVERING OUR IMAGINATION

49

FINDING OUT WHAT WE CAN DO

A Ugandan friend once said to me, 'we should get to know people slowly'. It was an unusual remark and set me thinking how quickly we so often categorise people! American? So she supports Bush. Nigerian? So he is a crook. Zimbabwean? So she is infected with HIV. Mentally disabled? So he is useless. I was once answerable to a man who said to me, 'I thought you were disorganised, but I see you aren't.' I had no time to be angry at his quick judgment, so chuffed was I by his honesty.

In Chapter 9 of John's gospel we have this 'useless' beggar, blind from birth. He didn't even have the wit to ask to be cured. But he was cured anyway. The other gospel writers would have ended the story there, but not John. For him it was only Act I. We are told the man owned up when the bystanders questioned him; that he stood his ground when his parents deserted him; and, most of all, that he gave the Jewish leaders a lesson in logic to which they were unaccustomed. This man found himself through a process of facing each hurdle as it came. When the going got tough he could have backed off and said or done, 'what was expected of him'. A few smooth words, a little 'economy with the truth' would have got him out of a lot of trouble. This guy would have been passed a hundred times in the street and few would take any notice of him. Yet within him there was a courage waiting for the moment to show itself.

We do not know what we are capable of. But there is no harm in taking time to try to find out. In a recent anthology of prison writings, *Conscience be my Guide*,[1] Lovemore Madhuku, [then] chairman of the National Constitutional Assembly in Zimbabwe, says at one point, 'I soon found that I had crossed the threshold of fear in the sense that I became strong through resisting'. There is no boasting in that statement. It is simply an expression of an experience with which the once blind man could resonate. I do not know what I am capable of until I move beyond my quiet life. The poet Robert Browning wrote, 'Ah, but a man's reach should exceed his grasp, or what is heaven for?' We are called to 'put out into the deep.' (Luke 5:4)

6 March, 2005

---

1 *Conscience be my Guide* edited by Geoffrey Bould. Weaver Press, Harare, 2005.

50

SUBSIDIARITY

Winston Churchill said something to the effect that democracy was a poor form of government but it is the best we've got. What is it about democracy that makes even those who do not practice it, invoke it? The former East Germany was called the German Democratic Republic. North Korea calls itself something similar,[1] and closer to home the Congo has adopted the same adjective.[2]

The attraction lies in the sense that we, the people, have a say in the making of decisions that affect our lives. Greece is credited with the origin and the practice of the word but something similar is found in many cultures. In Zimbabwe neither the village *dare* among the Shona nor the *indaba* among the Ndebele were rubber stamps. The leader who did not seek consensus was soon in trouble.

It was when civic entities grew in size that leaders became able to ignore the interests of small groups. In the empires of ancient Rome, medieval Europe and modern America, the small group counted for little. Leaders could ignore them because they could easily counterbalance any whisper of complaint by the weight of 'the majority'. The trouble is that modern democracy has not really changed this. With or without a vote, the majority can ride roughshod over the little people. 'Majority rule' is not a

---

.. The Democratic People's Republic of Korea.

2   The Democratic Republic of the Congo.

panacea for all ills. Ask the Tonga people of Zimbabwe! They were displaced in the 1950s without their consent and are still waiting today, after 25 years of putative democracy, for some meaningful rehabilitation.

Perhaps we can say that democracy simply does not work unless it finds some mechanism to be attentive to the most marginalised in society. It could be an ethnic group like the Tonga, or a group marginalised by their medical condition like those who are mentally disabled.

The church claims a mission to be the salt of the nations (Matt 5:13) but it has taken centuries to move from metaphor to practice. Still, there were many positive signs in the twentieth century that she was beginning to take this task seriously. One that is *à propos* here is the principle of subsidiarity put forward by Pope Pius X1 in 1931. Simply stated, it says that no organisation (such as a government) should take on itself tasks that can be performed by bodies smaller that itself (e.g. local councils). This is not just a minor adjustment of the body politic. It is a fundamental principle of human nature, which enables people to have a voice at their level. In other words it is a way of respecting the dynamics of the *dare* while recognising the inevitability of national governments. Churchill would have approved.

14 March, 2005

51

ADMITTING MISTAKES

'The world we were born into has gone. We shall never completely recapture its climate, its seasons, the way its plants grew and its animals lived. This is not a wild-eyed prediction. Respectable science knows it and says it. Nine of the world's ten warmest years since records were kept have occurred in the past fourteen years. Who is responsible? We are. Can we moderate climate change, slow it down, and eventually reverse it? Yes – if we try.' This notice for a book, *The Overheating World*, appeared in the *New York Review of Books* (October 2003).

Can we reverse global warming? Can we reduce global poverty? Can we heal the wounds of Zimbabwe? Yes – if *we* try – that means all of us together. But what is it that makes it so difficult for us to put our joint wills into gear and set about trying? Too often, we – or some of us – create scapegoats. Our problems are the fault of the Americans, the World Bank, Tony Blair ... When are we going to reach the point where we say it is our fault? We have made mistakes. We are responsible. Surely it is only very small children who cry, 'It wasn't me, it was ...'.

Recently unearthed footage of the Kennedy[1] years show the president admitting on television a few days after the Bay of Pigs,[2]

---

1   President John F. Kennedy (nicknamed JFK), was an American politician who served as the 35th President of the United States from January 1961 until his assassination in November 1963.
2   A failed military invasion of Cuba by a para-military group sponsored by the United States in 1961.

'I made a mistake.' Why is it so awesome to watch a president admit he was wrong? It must be because it is such a rare event. Literally it requires a conversion, a turn-around of heart and will. It requires a quality we call 'humility'. It is rare but we are all called to it.

'I cannot understand my own behaviour. I fail to carry out the things I want to do, and I find myself doing the very things I hate,' (Romans 7:15). Recognition of our darkness within is a first step. If we are Christians we have just accompanied Jesus on his inexorable journey to death. Those who brought about his destruction just would not try to understand, would not make any kind of first step. They were completely caught up in their own selfish agendas and did not even have the desire to look at the situation honestly. We say we would never have behaved as our ancestors did. But is this really true?

The poet Gerard Manley Hopkins desired that the Lord would 'Easter in us'. The early disciples were completely changed by the resurrection. From being stuck in their own narrow self-absorbed world they moved out to proclaim openly the Easter message. They knew 'that neither you nor your leaders had any idea what you were really doing' (Acts 3:17). But now it is wake-up time. It is time to look at our world – globally and locally – and try to 'restore the ruined houses,' (Isaiah 58:12).

29 March, 2005

52

WAITING FOR WHAT?

A little beyond Chegutu the bus died. It belonged to a company called 'Tombs' and one wondered if there was a connection. Some left the bus and started hitching. Others stood around the bus and still others remained seated. The engine covering was removed and work began on tracing the fault. A little later a second bus arrived, pulled in and took on board as many of us as could squeeze in, standing in the aisle. We reached our destination safely if a little frayed.

Reflecting on the incident it was noticeable that not a word was said in explanation or apology. And no one seemed to expect either. It was as though this is all quite normal. One starts the day with certain simple expectations. But anything, ANYTHING, can happen along the way. If it does, you simply adjust. You don't ask. You don't make demands. You just hope for the best. Sometimes, as in this event, you are lucky and an alternative way is provided. But sometimes you are just left and have to make do as best you can.

For weeks we have lived through a crisis. Many words have been written but there are no real explanations. Many photos have been displayed but no apologies. What is striking is that we do not even expect an explanation, much less an apology. Yes, there have been many 'explanations,' but none of them convincing. There have even been some mild words of regret but they only seem to rise from a sense of having been caught out.

We battle in our minds to understand ourselves. Who are we? Is there such a thing as a Zimbabwean identity? This inability to hold people accountable, where does it come from? Do we sense that if we stand up, like Oliver Twist,[1] and make demands we will have to bear the consequences alone? Do we have any real sense of solidarity among ourselves such that if one is in need another will help? I have heard it said that Zimbabweans abroad tend to just get on with their own lives. They are not known for supporting one another as other nationalities do. Is this true? They do not have great expectations that solidarity will deliver anything.

Again and again we come back to the lessons our present experience teaches. It is a path strewn with opportunities for reflection. It is not a time to just passively wait for another bus to come along. It may. But it may not and then we will be left standing at the side of the road looking pretty foolish while the rest of the world rushes by. Tanzania is not usually considered one of the strong economies of Africa and yet, in 34 years of independence, they have yet to discover what a fuel queue is.

24 July, 2005

---

1   Oliver Twist is the hero of the novel bearing the same name by Charles Dickens, and first published as a serial 1837–39. The story is of the orphan Oliver Twist, who begins life in a workhouse and is then sold into apprenticeship with an undertaker. He escapes and travels to London, where he meets the Artful Dodger, a member of a gang of juvenile pickpockets led by the elderly criminal, Fagin. The novel is notable for its unromantic portrayal of criminals, as well as for exposing the cruel treatment of the many orphans in London in the mid-19th century. Dickens satirises the hypocrisies of his time, including child labour, the recruitment of children as criminals, and the presence of street children.

53

FEAR DRIVEN OUT

In love there can be no fear,
For fear is driven out by perfect love.
I John 4: 18

These familiar words can anaesthetise us. We become oblivious to their meaning. Fear is a weapon used by every tyrant and schoolboy bully. It is a way of imposing your will on another. Its grosser forms exist all around us, but its subtler forms also abound in organisations, workplaces and families. It is the one great negative which paralyses us.

For months, even years, we have seen it take over our society. How many times is a statement quoted followed by the words 'who declined to give his name for fear of victimisation'? It was astonishing recently to see even the government claiming anonymity. A report from the *Sunday Times* (SA) read, "'the President's position is that his government will simply not accept the loan if it has rigid conditions....'' said the minister who declined to be named.'

You, the reader, might well respond, 'well, you are not exactly forthcoming about your name.' That is true, yet lots of papers go in for pseudonyms. I think it is partly not to distract the reader! Whatever the reason I like to think, in my case at least, it is not due to fear! But of course I may be deceiving myself.

Anyway, the point is fear is endemic in our society. When

you are rooted in fear all you try to do is survive. There is no room for creativity or building for the future. In a much more extreme situation than ours Viktor Frankl wrote of conditions in a concentration camp:

> ...*everything that was not connected with the immediate task of keeping oneself and one's closest friends alive lost its value. Everything was sacrificed to this end. A man's character became involved to the point that he was caught in a mental turmoil which threatened all the values he held and threw them into doubt.*[1]

Our situation may not be so desperate but some of the symptoms are there. People's values, culture, ways of relating to each other – all go on 'hold' as they struggle to survive one more day. Driven from Epworth to Caledonia and from Caledonia to where. And all the time a person lives in fear of what might happen next.

Yet in the depths of his suffering in the Auschwitz camp, Frankl was still able to write:

> *A thought transfixed me: for the first time in my life I saw the truth as it is set into song by so many poets, proclaimed as the final wisdom by so many thinkers. The truth – that love is the ultimate and highest goal to which man can aspire. Then I grasped the meaning of the greatest secret that human poetry and human thought and belief have to impart: the salvation of man is through love and in love.*[2]

10 August, 2005

---

1   *Man's Search for Meaning*, p. 49. First published in 1946. It is now available as a PDF file off the web.
2   Ibid. p. 36.

54

'I WAS WRONG'

The category five hurricane that just missed a direct hit on America's 'Big Easy' – the city of New Orleans in Louisiana – prompts some sober reflections.

First, there is the achievement of evacuating a whole city that was going about its business under clear blue skies. Everyone had enough sense to ignore the seeming normality and heed the weather people. If Katrina had come a century ago, or even 50 years ago, there would have been no such warning and hundreds of thousands would have perished.

Then there is the marvel of a city below sea level, not far inland like Jericho (260 meters below sea level), but right next to the Gulf of Mexico. The French, who ran this part of the world in the eighteenth century, built levees. These were raised embankments, against the Mississippi River, which empties into the Gulf, and Lake Pontchartrain, which lies north of the city. The levees buckled but they held – just.

Now the bad news. As New Orleans has grown and tamed the Mississippi it has eroded the marshlands and swampy delta. Silt and nutrients from the river's floods have been diverted and the concrete of a modern city have replaced the sprawling coastal wetlands that would have taken the brunt of the hurricane's attack. So humans are not quite so bright after all. While the city has been saved from total submersion, two of the levees have broken, flooding it. It will take four months to get New Orleans back on its feet.

We have that ability to combine advanced science and wondrous engineering with crass short-sightedness. Global warming is the single biggest threat to our grandchildren's livelihood. Scientists have piled up the data about greenhouse gases and ice-caps melting, but it all makes no difference to policy makers who just see profit margins as their top priority. They sacrifice everything to keep those graphs friendly. Their mind is made up. They don't want to be confused with facts.

Obduracy is an ancient vice. Pharaoh was good at it and he got a fair drowning as a result. But we have some practitioners in our own time and not very far from here. The opposite of Obduracy is humility; the ability to say 'I made a mistake.' President John F Kennedy said just that after the Bay of Pigs disaster. For the most powerful person in the world to say, 'I was wrong,' is refreshing. Now, if only one or two powerful people in our country could say that...

31 August, 2005

55

'I WANT TO SEE THE MANAGER.'

Our President is in Cuba where he has described himself as a 'fellow revolutionary' with his host. It is not clear what this title conveys. Fidel Castro presides over a country with limited human freedoms but people are fed and educated, and health services are available to all. Can the same be said about our country? The title elevates perception over reality, form over substance. As we continue to survey the devastation around us I am reminded of my grandmother. She had a rather formidable way of shopping and when she judged the quality of the product, or the service, to be below standard she had a way of announcing she wanted to 'see the manager'. Shop assistants would tremble and scurry away and prepare their explanations and even the manager would approach as respectful as a *mukuwasha* before his *ambuya*, and he would ensure that whatever had gone wrong was put right. Professional standards mattered.

That was another place and another time. To dream of holding our public servants to account today and in our land is to do just that – to dream. And yet it is the foundation of sound society. Until we, the public, begin to demand service we will continue to be seen as of little account. We are, after all, paying their salaries with our taxes.

And, while speaking of people of little account, Jean Vanier, a Canadian who has devoted his life to founding communities for people with mental disabilities, tells the story of how his father taught him to respect those 'under' him. The elder Vanier, who went on to represent the Queen as head of state in Canada, received a report from the navy where his son, Jean was training. Jean, the report said, did not show enough respect for his superiors. Georges Vanier remarked, 'I would be much more concerned if he did not show respect for his inferiors.'

What is it that has created the culture among us that allows anyone in public office, or any office, to feel they can lord it over the public who come asking a service? It is so much at variance with the old traditions where elaborate forms of respect were in place. To be a revolutionary, you don't have to reach for an AK47. You just have to ask to see the manager – and hold them to account.

14 September, 2005

56

TOUCHING MEMORY

A recent report of the President's visit to Rome spoke of the outrage of the British and Americans at the presence of one who 'has created hunger and poverty in his own country' coming to discuss world hunger. But the writer goes on to tell us that other delegates 'repeatedly applauded Mr Mugabe's fiery anti-western diatribe.'

In the long crisis of Zimbabwe this applause has been a constant backdrop. The President is seen as one who puts into words the enduring feelings of frustration of people in poor countries. Present realities do not wipe out painful memories. The oppression and exploitation of Africa by colonial powers may now be history but it is sharply remembered. And the feeling persists that it is still there in the attitudes of the decision-makers of the rich world. The drawn out agony of Iraq neatly summarises it: it is simply assumed that the Iraqis welcome the invasion of their country and the removal of their dictator.

The story is told that when the Irish nationalist leader, Michael Collins, arrived at Dublin Castle for the formal handover at the time of independence, and it is said that the British Governor complained, 'Mr Collins, you're seven minutes late.' Collins is said replied, 'we've been waiting seven hundred years. You can wait seven minutes.' Whether legend or fact the incident points to the place of memory in politics. Too much analysis focuses on the present – full of injustice though it may be. Someone once said that those who do not study the lessons of history are doomed to repeat its mistakes.

The popularity of Mr Mugabe in many developing countries is a fact. It may be extremely irritating to the Zimbabwean queuing for sugar or diesel, or very upsetting to someone who has lost their home or been subjected to electoral violence, but the man is applauded. He is seen as giving a voice to those who do not have one. He expresses feelings coming from the memories of people who were repressed for too long. The fact that in his own country he is not actually doing anything to help his own people rise out of oppression – quite the contrary – is brushed aside.

Remembering defines who we are and every form of culture – secular and religious – recognises this. We have Heroes' Acre and we also have the Passover 'to remind you' (Exodus 12:14). In Christian faith the Eucharist is a central act of worship 'in memory of me' (I Corinthians 11: 25). Remembering those things that build us up, gives identity and purpose to life. Failing to deal with painful memories – individual or collective (such as Gukurahundi) – diminishes us.

25 October, 2005

57

OWNERSHIP

I once bought some Christmas presents for a family in Mhondoro. I put some thought into 'what' for 'who', but not into the method of distribution. I started with the youngest (now a successful businessman) who shrieked with joy over his gift. I then moved on to the second youngest which produced screams of frustration from the youngest who saw no reason why he shouldn't receive that present as well.

Owning things is one of the joys of life and is written into the book of Genesis where we are told God gave us the earth. Maybe the third word we learn after 'mai' and 'baba' is 'mine'. New shoes, a new dress or a new house give immense pleasure. The trouble with ownership is that it carries some implications.

I met a man from a foreign country who worked in forestry in a neighbouring state for fifteen years. He studied the trees that were suitable there; he worked out conservation measures that were enforced by 'forestry police' and he advocated regular replanting. He trained a team of colleagues. When he left he felt he had done something really useful for the country.

That was 25 years ago. Now he says he has heard from those colleagues that none of the measures he taught were followed. The place where he put in such hard work is a desert. The people have to travel six to eight kilometres to find firewood. He is not bitter but he is disappointed. He says, 'perhaps we imposed our ways?'

He is almost certainly right. People will never 'own' what they are forced to do. We lament the collapse of the water system in Harare, the ecological devastation in the countryside and the failure of maintenance in our power plants and even Kariba Dam. But it all comes down to ownership. Why worry about something that you do not own?

People did not 'own' Zimbabwe in the bad old days before independence. But even since 1980 there has been little sense of 'ownership' of the country even though lip service is paid to the new owners of land. The basis of real ownership is secure title. And who can have that when you can be thrown off your land or out of your house at any moment.

We can never get tired of saying that the basis of secure title is an inviolable constitution which binds everyone and which can only be changed with the consent of the citizens.

My little friend had to learn that, while he had his present, others were entitled to theirs too.

24 November, 2005

58

KNOW WHERE YOU COME FROM

Fay Chung, who was active in the liberation struggle in Mozambique and later in establishing imaginative initiatives in education in the new Zimbabwe, has written an account of her experiences. Her book, *Re-living the Second Chimurenga*,[1] was launched at the Book Café in Harare in early February in the form of a debate between herself and Wilfred Mhanda who also played a prominent role in the struggle (known as Cde Dzino). It was a charged occasion because the two protagonists were joined by a number of others who either experienced the struggle themselves or were familiar with it second-hand.

What came out of the cut and thrust of the evening was that different people have their own 'truth' about what happened and we are still at a subjective stage of really understanding the history of that time. We are too near to it and feelings are still too sensitive for us to really know.

At the same time it emerged that some people prominent in public life today want to hide their involvement in the war and are annoyed when their role is mentioned. No explanation for this was offered but it could be that the ideals of that time are so different from the ideals of the present that their recall is irritating. Others, especially younger people – the 'born-frees' – are confused about it. They are constantly reminded of the

---

1   *Re-living the Second Chimurenga: Memories from Zimbabwe's Liberation Struggle.* Weaver Press, Harare, 2007.

glorious struggle for freedom but they see little of its fruits today. As one speaker put it, 'people in those days were committed to an ideal and were willing to sacrifice everything – their comfort, their education, even their lives. We can't ask people today to be committed because they don't know what they are supposed to be committed to.' It is a bleak scenario.

Fay Chung was warmly congratulated for opening a new furrow. She was cited as being the first to set down her experiences and the fervent hope was repeatedly expressed that others would also do the same. A number of speakers pointed to mistakes –some serious – in her writing but all acknowledged that a debate was now open. Many terrible things happened in the war but at root it was driven by a passionate desire to sacrifice everything for the sake of freedom and dignity. Another word for this is love. 'A person can have no greater love than to lay down their life for their friends' (John 15:13). It has often been said that war brings out the best in human beings. It also brings out the worst and this was openly acknowledged at the launch.

3 February, 2006

59

REACHING OUT TO OTHERS

Eric Worby, writing in *Zimbabwe's Unfinished Business*, describes how, on 23 July, 2002, President Mugabe opened the third session of the fifth parliament of Zimbabwe. 'Streets leading to the city centre were blockaded, cars searched, and demonstrators and suspected supporters of the opposition banned.'

On the same chilly afternoon, he continues, 200 workers on Leopardvlei Farm, in Central Mashonaland, were ordered out of their compound by the new owner, Reward Marufu, the President's brother-in-law; their houses were burned and they were ordered to leave. Effectively, they were banned.

Back in Harare the opposition walked out of Parliament refusing to recognise the legitimacy of the recently held elections. They were doing their best to 'ban' the President. And then, Worby concludes, the US and the EU banned senior Zimbabwe leaders from travelling to their countries.

To ban, exile, displace, ostracise, outlaw or scapegoat are all exercises of different degrees of violence, long practised in Rhodesia and Zimbabwe. They are tacit admissions of failure to engage, dialogue, include, tolerate or integrate. The discriminatory laws of the 1920s and 1930s, which divided up land, jobs, laws, sport, housing and schools created habits of mind that survived the hoisting of our multi-coloured flag on the 18 April, 1980. To this day we live in a deeply divided land where those on the 'inside' enjoy wealth and power to the exclusion of the majority on the 'outside' who are effectively banned from living a life of health and dignity. To grow crops, to sell produce, to find school fees, to obtain medicine or just to find somewhere to live - all of these are major energy draining activities. They are the daily life of the banned.

Is it possible that we could just open our eyes and stop banning each other and enter into some kind of dialogue for the good of everyone? Is it possible to leave judgments aside for a while and reach out to one another? We will get absolutely nowhere if we continue with bitterness and division. 'If you are bringing your offering to the altar and there remember that your brother has something against you, leave your offering there before the altar, go and be reconciled with your brother first, and then come back and present your offering.' (Matthew 5:23)

8 February, 2006

60

OUR DEATH AND OUR RISING

In 1966, in the months after UDI, there was much discussion about the closing of the Feruca fuel pipeline from Beira to Mutare as a result of sanctions against Ian Smith's regime. In 2006, 40 years later, donkeys cross the mountains from Mozambique laden with containers of the same precious liquid. True, the economy is not totally dependent on donkeys, not yet anyway. But these patient animals, which have served us for millennia, could be symbols of where we are.

The French have a saying, *reculer pour mieux sauter* (take a step back so as to make a better jump). The saying commends the practice. If you travel the growth points of Zimbabwe – a growth point is not quite a town but it is much more than a 'business centre' – you will often notice, even today, vibrant small industries. You will see people with small homemade welding machines making ploughshares, hoes and sickles, scotch carts, school tables and chairs. Sometimes they employ up to eleven workers. Others make shoes and handbags or school bags 'for the Indian shops'. Where there is an enabling environment people are very creative and industrious. Their industry is at an earlier stage than the one that produces tractors and combined harvesters but perhaps it is better founded.

And what is true of the economic life of people could also be true of their politics. Small communities, women's groups, residents associations, burial societies and similar civic groups are discovering how to order their affairs and find their voice. The grant politics of sovereignty and liberation, that may have served us for a time after independence, is now giving way at the grassroots to something much more modest but also more solid.

Christians call this time of the year 'Lent', a word that perhaps comes from the len(gh)t(ening) of the days (in the northern hemisphere). It is time of preparation for celebrating the mysteries of Jesus's death and rising. This means that it is a time for reflecting on our own 'death' and our own 'rising' as persons and as a country. The first stage is death. That is where we are now in Zimbabwe. There is a kind of death of the vast dreams and longings of the first years of independence. There is a passion and a kind of death in every person's life one way or another. And the same can be true of a community – even as big a community as a country. But the more we live that process positively and searchingly – even if it means going back a step or two – the more we prepare the resurrection. And, by the way, when Jesus entered Jerusalem he was riding a donkey.

22 March, 2006

61

DESIRE

'There is no great desire to save the planet, just as there is no huge desire to bring about justice and eliminate poverty.' This matter-of-fact observation by José González Faus, in a booklet called *The Kyoto Horizon*,[1] starkly describes our dilemma. We have all the means at hand to eliminate poverty and preserve our planet but we don't want to. The first recorded words of Jesus in John's Gospel are, 'what do you want?' (1:38). The disciples seem to have been astonished by this question. Perhaps they had never been asked such a thing before. What do we want? What do I want?

Wise people tell us to 'get in touch with your desires,' by which they mean listen to what is deepest within you and, once you have named it, move towards it steadily. This device proposes no easy answer. At first I might answer I want a profession, a house, a car, an intimate relationship and a host of other things. I want certain things for my life – individual personal things. I leave community and global needs to politicians. I leave the poor and the ozone layer to them.

But it is rare for a politician to move ahead of his constituents. It is the mark of great leadership and it is not often we see the likes of them. A leader's instinct bids him or her to move only at the pace of those who elected them. They know we are dangerously

---

1 *The Kyoto Horizon: The Problem of the Environment* by Joan Carrera and José I. González Faus available on <https://www.cristianismeijusticia.net/files/en122.pdf>

near a point of no return in global warming and they would like to do something about it, but the individuals who chose them will not tolerate any diminishment of their standard of living. So nothing happens. What they know is right and would really like to do becomes smothered in phrases about 'politics being the art of the possible'.

I still want to believe that our Zimbabwe government would like to eradicate poverty and improve the lives of people. But at the end of the day this desire is smothered under a stronger, more selfish desire to simply stay in power and 'enjoy its fruits'. If the common good could be served at the same time, that would be fine. But if it can't, well, that's just too bad. In 1980, the new government acquired a country where the Zimbabwe dollar was slightly stronger than the US dollar. Today we have a worthless currency, hyper-inflation and a huge external debt. Those who lead us seem more concerned to make money for themselves than to run the country efficiently and for the good of the people. The question we must ask is how do we move forward and out of this huge poverty trap where the rich get richer and the poor poorer?

Perhaps the answer is that we do not want to eliminate poverty just as we do not want to save our planet.

6 July, 2006

62

SILENT VOICES

L ast week a book was launched in Harare about the struggle of minority language groups in Zimbabwe to have their languages taught to their children in their schools. The keynote speaker arrived for his first day of school 25 years ago to discover only English and Ndebele were spoken. He is a Tonga. The book is called *Silent Voices*.[1] This event was in the back of my mind when a colleague told me of a meeting yesterday about development in Zimbabwe. There are many organisations wanting to contribute to the growth of our country. The problem is bureaucracy. If you want to do something with your own resources you have to have an 'understanding' with the relevant ministry, local government office and party officials. In the end you can be so overwhelmed by the 'red tape' that you give up. Someone said to the government officials at the meeting, 'you are treating us as enemies, not as partners'.

The reply given was that 'you people' are always bringing in politics. This charge, thrown at development workers, church leaders and anyone who says anything about the present situation, is an expression of fear. It is true that politics are involved; the price of bread, the slashing of zeros, the availability of fuel, the rise of school fees – all of these are 'politics'. What is wrong with 'bringing in politics'. It is the air we breathe. It is the

---

1   *Silent Voices: Indigenous Languages in Zimbabwe.* A report compiled by Isaac Mumpande. Silveira House and Weaver Press, Harare. 2006.

sign of a scared government when it gets worried when people ask questions. Or that wants to have endless 'understandings'.

The ordinary life of people is boxed in by restrictions and in their desperation people turn on each other. Since those above squeeze us, we squeeze those below. When someone dies – and many are dying these days – relatives are easy prey. You have to get the body out of the mortuary. You have to buy a coffin. You have to buy a grave. It is a seller's market. The seller is tempted to push the price as high as it will go. Fairness, equity, justice. What are they? There is the story of the boss who shouts at his worker. The worker is afraid to reply so he bottles up his frustration inside only to release it on his wife when he gets home. She is shocked but afraid to answer him back and shouts at their child. He is hurt but swallows his anger and goes out and kicks the dog, which chases the cat and a mouse dies that day.

So there is always the tendency to transfer our anger to 'softer' targets. But something has been happening these six long years. People are interrupting the transfer sequence. They are finding their voice. They are no longer silent. They are speaking up directly against those who constantly call for submission. They are challenging the climate of control and heartlessness prevalent in government structures. Media reports abroad often report the apparently hopeless situation in Zimbabwe. It is far from hopeless. People are wide-awake, searching, questioning struggling and speaking. It is only a matter of time before the new struggle for freedom, a deeper one than the former, gives birth.

23 August, 2006

63

SOLDIERING ON

Speaking to journalists on 13 July at Zimbabwe House, President Mugabe was reported in *The Herald* as being 'aware of the hardships people were going through'.The government, he said, was going flat out to turn around the economy.

On the last day of the same month we have one of the government's 'flat out' actions; slashing three zeroes from our bank notes. A report by Reuters news agency suggests a problem with informing us what exactly this means. 'Our currency is in trouble. Our people are experiencing incredible hardships and inconveniences associated with too many zeroes,' Central Bank Governor Gideon Gono said. 'All monetary values ... have been re-based by striking out three zeroes.' Anonymous economists said the step 'did not amount to a revaluation but was aimed at making it easier for consumers to handle increasingly unwieldy wads of banknotes.'

But the same news agency gave us another report on the same day, 'Zimbabwe's central bank devalued its dollar by 60 percent [today] after announcing it had decided to knock three zeroes off all banknotes to help consumers deal with hyperinflation of nearly 1,200 percent. "With immediate effect the interbank exchange rate has been adjusted," Gono said in a televised address'

So the operation has been variously called a 're-basing,' 'not a revaluation,' 'a devaluation,' 'an adjustment' and even a 'redenominating.' What is the man and woman in the street supposed to make of it? The key phrase behind all this was in the President's words to the journalists on 13 July, 'we have decided to soldier on.' The phrase comes from wartime when the troops are not making an impact and no one quite knows what will happen next. There is no clear strategy and the enemy's whereabouts are unknown. The only thing to do is to keep going even if we don't know where. To say 'we have decided' implies there is a choice but there is no choice for anyone other than the speaker who seems to be using 'we' in the royal sense; I have decided.

And when it comes to royalty we remember King David ordered a census (2 Samuel 24) and came up with the figure of 1,300,000 armed men. Commentators say we should probably slash a couple of zeroes from the number. Anyway, the king was punished by God – or rather the people were . in three days of pestilence, 70 000 died. The king was not supposed to calculate his own strength but rely on God. His decision brought misery to families.

1 August, 2006

64

DEATH SENTENCE

Prison is, by definition, a place where people are held. Their freedom is taken away. Originally it was a way of preventing someone from harming others without actually killing him or her. Gradually prevention moved to punishment and retribution was added to the reasons for seizing someone by force.

But now in many countries there is a third aim – rehabilitation: the desire to help a person re-enter normal life with a changed outlook. Great efforts are made to accompany a person in prison with counselling, spiritual care and skills training. We can be thankful that society, at least in its better moments, has moved on to such a noble desire.

But rehabilitation requires resources – human and financial – and Zimbabwe does not spend its money on such services, though the word 'service' does appear: ours is officially the 'Zimbabwe Prison Service.' That's a start.

But how does the death sentence fit into 'rehabilitation'? Is it an admission that we have failed on earth and we leave it to heaven to do the rehabilitating? One of the reasons why the death penalty is so distasteful to many societies today is that we sense we have no right to take away the life of another – no matter what the crime. We may be able to prove in court that this person did this thing but even then there can be room for doubt. In the UK in the 1980s there were unsound convictions for the so-called Birmingham Six[1] and the Guildford Four.[2] There was pressure on state institutions at the time to be seen to be doing something about the IRA 'terrorists'. After exhaustive and exhausting campaigns the prisoners were released and their sentences were quashed.

But even if convictions are sound can we really know the motives of a criminal? During the time reviewed by the Truth and Reconciliation Commission in South Africa, 2,500 people were hanged; 95% were black and 100% of those who condemned them were white. Is it likely that the judges really understood the motives of those they condemned? One might argue that was an unjust state. Where then is there a just state? Texas?

One of the attractions writers work on in murder stories is how they 'help us see what we don't understand.'[3] This suggestion was made by Colin Burrow who brings light relief into the search for motives by having an accused explain, 'This is why I did it: the peptides which control the level of greed in my body were at dangerously low levels, and owing to abnormalities in my hypothalamus my serotonin levels were low. Now do you understand?'

The key reason why taking another's life can no longer be justified is our growing understanding of human dignity. A human being is just too mysterious to be tampered with. The 'wonder of my being' (Psalm 139) is beyond the comprehension of another person.

13 September, 2006

---

1   Si. Irish men who were sentenced to life imprisonment in 1975 in England for the Birmingham pub bombings. Their convictions were declared unjust and unsatisfactory and quashed by the Court of Appeal on 14 March 1991.

2   The Guildford Four was a collective name for a group whose convictions in English courts in 1975 for the Guildford pub bombings of 5 October 1974 were eventually quashed after long campaigns for justice.

3   'You, Your Bow and the Gods. by Colin Burrow. *London Review of Books*, 27:18, 22 September, 2005.

65

CIVIL SOCIETY IN THE LEAD

'In war, the first casualty is truth.' This perception was first expressed by the Greek tragic dramatist, Aeschylus (525-426 BC). Approximately 2,400 years later, the economist Wellington Chadehumbe said something similar in the *Zimbabwe Independent*[1] that 'truth is a driver of growth'. Where there is no truth there is no development. The struggle for freedom called for much rhetoric and action but the struggle for development calls for 'measured words of wisdom... it has no value if it does not expand freedoms.' Chadehumbe believes that freedom for a country 'must percolate through society and trickle down to the individual.' Only free individuals can develop a society. '... leadership is at its quintessence when the key tools it employs are inspiration and vision as opposed to threats and intimidation.' In other words, people will only act effectively when they believe what they are doing is right and true.

Goran Hyden, a political scientist, has written that 30 years ago 'the state was viewed as the engine that would make a positive difference in the lives of people... [it was believed to be] capable of ensuring the security and welfare of citizens.' Alas, no longer! 'The bubble of popular expectations about development that characterised the 1970s has been burst...' Now it is civil society that is in the driving seat. In the past three decades there has been a loss of confidence in the state and a growth in the

---

1   1-7 September, 2006.

power of public opinion. The *New York Times* even called it a 'second superpower.' In other words, public opinion is a far better repository of what is true and what is false than governments. Tony Blair[2] twists and turns to try and convince people 'it was right' to invade Iraq but fewer and fewer people are convinced. In the end he is powerless and will soon have to go.

All of this is music to our ears. The writing is on the wall for those who try to force their truth upon us. Whatever despondency and pain we may feel about our situation, civil society today in Zimbabwe is far healthier than it has ever been. Thanks to a whole cluster of reasons, one of which must be the expansion of education opportunities in the 1980s, people today have a strong sense of what is true and what is false. And they know too, more than ever before, what they really want of the state. At the moment opportunities are denied, blocked, frustrated. Expressions of opinion by civil society are brutally suppressed. It is all painfully reminiscent of the cruelty of the South African government in the late 1980s just before the dawn. But dawn there was – and dawn here too there will be. It would be naive to invest civil society with some kind of infallibility. No doubt there will always be greed and foolishness among its prophets and artisans. Yet the general thrust remains; a healthy groundswell of people finding their voice, a voice that that will be the master, not the slave, of governments.

19 September, 2006.

---

2   Prime Minister of Great Britain 1997-2007. Despite strong public feeling and much criticism, in 2003 Blair decided to enter the Iraq war in support of the USA. In doing so he manipulated the facts to justify his decision.

66

THE POWER OF IMAGINATION

This slogan from the student protests in Paris in 1968 came to mind when I read two articles on Zimbabwe in the past week – one from within the country, one from without. Eldred Masunungure, from the University of Zimbabwe, calls us a 'risk-averse' people.[1] We have been subjugated for so long – in the colonial years and latterly by our own government – we have become used to subjugation. We have learnt that taking risks to obtain freedom doesn't bring results. So we have given up. Anyone who calls us into the streets will have little success. For the vast majority it literally isn't worth the risk. Better to just wait for better times.

Masunungure detects something even more debilitating below the surface. We now accept the abnormal as normal. (He credits Jonathan Moyo with inventing this phrase.) He points to the constant Zimbabwe habit of diffusing anger by joking about adversity, a habit which 'creates and inculcates fatalistic or defeatist values in our society,' presently and for future generations. We are 'immobilising ourselves. When ZESA cuts our power, says Masunungure, or the City Council denies us water, we don't get angry, we just buy a generator or sink a borehole. If we can't afford these, we buy candles and draw water from unprotected wells. But the last thing we think of is a focused

---

1   'Zimbabwe: Why Zimbabweans Will Not Revolt Against Authority' by Eldred Masunungure. *The Standard*, 1/10/2006.

collective response.

On the other hand, he says, the government is a master at taking risks. They learnt it from Ian Smith whose gamble in 1965 paid off at least in the short term. The land grab and Murambatsvina were simply the most high profile of a succession of risks taken by the present government. And the risks paid off. No one responded effectively. The government has been strong, pro-active and unpredictable while the people have been over-awed, cowed and at a loss as to what to do.

The second article comes from a Ghanaian, George Ayittey, of the American University in Washington, and gives some kind of answer. He begins by saying the recent ZCTU protest was 'to put it mildly, dumb. While he sympathises with the protesters, he says they need a 'good talking to' because they 'continually repeat old stupid mistakes'. Perhaps his criticism is deliberately harsh so as to rouse his readers. But what does he advise? 'There are better ways of fighting a tyrannical regime and they require a huge dose of the imagination and learning from the experience of other countries. He quotes a number of examples from Africa but there is one from Asia, which he could also have mentioned.

Gandhi hoped for the freedom of India in the 1920s but the struggle became bogged down in frustrations on every side. He used to go into retreat to reflect and ponder how to move the process forward non-violently. The British had, however, imposed a salt tax, which was a burden for the ordinary people. Gandhi emerged from his retreat to lead a march to the sea where he invited them to help themselves to all the salt they wanted. They gathered it free and without tax. Now, it is true that in Zimbabwe any kind of marching attracts government attention but it is not the march itself but the imagination behind it that catches attention.

5 October, 2006

67

AWAKE TO GOD

I recently saw a film about the last days of Hitler. The dictator is in his bunker below Berlin moving imaginary armies around a map in a final effort to save Germany from defeat. The camera moves to the faces of the generals who surround the table and shows their total disbelief. When one of them tries to tell the leader 'there are no armies left,' Hitler rants at them. Reserve Bank Governor Gideon Gono is no Hitler but he is good at ceaseless activity, which does everything except actually face the reality. On the same day as *The Herald* covered its front page with his latest moves, there was another report reminding us that the World Bank considers our economic crisis 'the worst in the world outside a war zone.'

A small group of people last week invited Archbishop Pius Ncube to talk to them about what the Church could do in Zimbabwe to help resolve the crisis. What was striking was his total honesty in the face of the situation. He simply said, 'we don't know what to do. In different ways he repeated the same message: there is no leadership, the 'opposition' is infiltrated and divided. We don't know what to do. You come to a meeting hoping for some inspiration and you go away empty and desolate. But at least it is the truth.

Filling our news pages and screens with activity to create a sense of measures taken to solve our problems is like treating people suffering from HIV and AIDS with Panadol. We are seen to be doing something but we are avoiding the real Issue. There is a story at the end of the tenth chapter of Luke's Gospel in which Jesus calls on some friends. They are two sisters and one of them begins preparing a meal, as any mother would do when a guest arrives. But she has a sister who is content to just sit by Jesus and listen to him. The busy sister complains but Jesus chides her gently and says, 'no, your sister here has chosen the right thing to do.'

We have pondered the story of Martha and Mary for two thousand years and still can't quite get inside it. We know Jesus is not condemning the work of Martha but he is saying that beyond work, beyond ceaseless activity, there is something more essential. And what is that? I cannot give a complete answer but it has to do with being quiet sometimes. It has to do with allowing reality to penetrate within me, listening to the cries of those who are suffering, attending to the heart of God who longs to heal this world but cannot do so unless invited.

11 October, 2006

68

THIRST FOR JUSTICE

'Justice delayed is justice denied' but still if eventually granted
it is 'better late than never.' *The Herald* (16 October) gave us
the good news about Judge President Rita Makarau's 'shock and
disbelief at discovering some inmates in Harare's remand prison
have been waiting up to *nine* years to be brought to trial. It is good
news because it is clear she is going to do something about it. She
'is determined to clear the backlog plaguing the High Court and
to decongest the prison to manageable levels and to a humanly
habitable degree. She went on to say, 'this is quite embarrassing
and disturbing. We should take full blame for this ordeal. We have
no excuse for this delay.'

Such honesty and resolve in high places is a breath of fresh
air and hopefully the approach will be contagious in other areas
of public life. We continue to look forward to huge changes that
will radically affect our decaying social and economic structures.
Perhaps we expect some velvet[1] or orange[2] revolution. that will
sweep away the old and give promise of a new beginning. Yet
things are unlikely to happen that way. What is more likely

1   The Velvet Revolution was so called because it was a non-violent transition
of power from dictatorship to democracy in the then Czechoslovakia. The period
of upheaval and transition took place from 17 November to 29 December, 1989.
2   The Orange Revolution took place from 22 November 2005 through to January 2006. 'Together, we are many! We cannot be defeated!' was the cry of the hundreds of thousands of citizens, wearing orange, who joined together in a powerful
civic movement, to stop the ruling elite from falsifying an election and hijacking
Ukraine's presidency.

is that people will change things – one person at a time. If the person who tries to make a difference is an influential person, like Justice Makarau, the change will have an immediate impact. But the lesson surely is that anyone in the country can wake up and say, 'this has to change'.

We are all accomplices, from the greatest to the least. Recently a group of young people received some capital and started a project to make bricks. All went well for a time but soon they became more interested in the fruits than in the work to produce them. They accepted an advance payment from a customer for making 10,000 bricks, made 6,000 and then sat back. No amount of cajoling made them budge and, short of legal proceedings that would be costly and uncertain, nothing could be done. The project collapsed and the young people are without a livelihood.

But let another person come and say, 'this is no way to conduct business,' and maybe the project will get a new start. The report in *The Herald* closes with a comment from the Justice, 'I have got fantastic support from my team and we are moving forward. Corruption may be contagious but honesty, enthusiasm and dedication are even more so.

18 October, 2006

69

STRENGTH OOZES BACK

One of my favourite proverbs expresses the wisdom that people are resilient. *Simba mukaka rinosinira*. No matter how much you draw, the milk seeps back. To the outside observer Zimbabwe may look like a drained reservoir at the end of the dry season. Seven years of evaporation has left us bereft of credit, skills, freedom and the necessities of life. Those seven years may look a hopeless wasteful descent into poverty and decay. But to the insider there are definite stages of movement, much of it positive. Nothing stands still.

There has been a noticeable shift from acceptance of control from the top (top down) to a demand for local initiative (bottom up). The government's gut reaction to any movement in society is to want to control it. During these seven lean years we have seen attempts at control extended not only to the election process but also to the media, the judiciary, the unions, the NGOs and other civic bodies. Whatever the thinking behind this, the desire to control seems to arise from a fear of people making their own decisions, which might eventually lead to the ruling party losing power.

Each of the seven years carries its own story. In the first years we saw much use of force to drive people off their property and attain the desired election results. In the middle years, attempts were made to channel finance and the economy in a desired direction, and more recently we have seen a further demonstration of force at the time of Murambatsvina, which is still continuing today.

But at the same time there is a quiet revolution in process and the government realises it and is even buying into it. People are starting their own organisations at the grassroots. These have nothing to do with politics but are simply for small- and medium-sized enterprises. While the government at first wanted to control these too – and even set up a Ministry to do this – they now realise that the best hope of growth is where the people themselves run their enterprises in the way they want. So the government has wisely backed off and even applauded the efforts of small entrepreneurs.

Another sign of strength returning is the way dialogue and inclusiveness are quietly taking the place of confrontation and exclusion; you are either with us or against us. In fact dialogue and inclusiveness are much more 'traditional' and 'cultural' than their opposites. In a distant rural area of the country recently a small community rejected a leader who thought he was in his position 'for life,' but they still retained him on the committee.

Before the seven lean years began people were content to enjoy the fat years – such as they were. They were not 'fat' for everyone. But now people are starting to appreciate that you cannot leave everything to government: each one has to take some responsibility for his or her life. And we are beginning to do it. Not long ago I visited the citizens of Hatcliffe Extension. They were frantically busy building their houses. I noticed that one lady, who was in the midst of cooking for the brick moulders, was growing a strawberry plant. Strawberries in Hatcliffe Extension!!

7 November, 2006

70

THE POWER OF IDEAS

'**O**ur society is infected by apathy, hypocrisy, petit bourgeois egotism, and hidden cruelty. The majority of the representatives of its upper stratum – the Party apparatus of the government and the highest, most successful layers of the intelligentsia – cling tenaciously to their open and secret privileges and are profoundly indifferent to the violations of human rights, the interests of progress, to the security and future of mankind.'

Who is writing and about what society? The reader may well recognise strong elements fitting a description of Zimbabwe today. In fact it is Andrei Sakharov, the Russian nuclear physicist who played a major part in developing the hydrogen bomb, writing in 1971 to Leonid Brezhnev, the ruler of the Soviet Union at the time. Sakharov started out as a privileged member of the Soviet elite but came to think his way out of the system and ended as one of its most effective critics. In his early life he put his whole heart and mind into giving the Soviets a weapon that would make them a world power. But he came to see that this power was going nowhere and he questioned it with the same energy he had used to build it.

Sakharov described the reality of life in the Soviet Union against the light of the international treaties that that same Union had signed. In particular, he pointed to the UN Declaration of Human Rights, shaming his government by pointing to the gap between the reality and its propaganda. As a result, the

KGB, Russia's secret service, became obsessed with Sakharov, devoting huge energy to tracking his every move and word. As the economy crumbled in the 1980s and their soldiers died in Afghanistan, fifteen busy old men in the Soviet politburo found time to discuss whether Sakharov's wife should be allowed to travel abroad for an eye operation.

What the Soviet leaders feared was the power of his ideas: 'the country's spiritual regeneration,' he wrote, 'demands the elimination of those conditions that drive people into hypocrisy and time-serving and that lead to feelings of impotence, discontent and disillusionment.' Sakharov and his fellow 'dissidents' represented a threat to the Soviet Union more powerful than the bomb he had helped to create. And in fact, despite the propaganda, the indoctrination in schools and universities and press restrictions, most educated Russians abandoned Marxism in the early 1990s, virtually overnight.

Ideas can harness energy and change society. But they have to be embodied in persons of integrity and courage. Do we have the ideas? Do we have the people?

22 November, 2006

71

KEEPING UP THE SPIRIT

People are tired. There is not even a hint of a solution to the problems facing the country. And the government does not seem to be interested. They are not embarrassed by inflation figures. They can't be because they do nothing about it. They are not troubled by the daily struggle of people. Perhaps they want it that way. People who are tired and exhausted are unlikely to protest.

So we are all getting used to it. There is even a danger we will loose the desire for a different state of things, though this is not possible no matter how trampled on people are. But there is the troubling parable of the eagle that grew up with chickens. It got used to pecking around in the yard with the chickens that never got further than stretching their wings. Life went on like that for a long time until one day a majestic eagle circled in the sky above and the chicken/eagle thought, 'I can do that too.' It made a few attempts to fly and got a few feet above the ground, but then got tired and gave up and sank back into the life it was used to.

Christmas is upon us and it is preceded in the Christian calendar by the time of Advent. Advent is all about hope – a word we easily use (I hope it rains) but which carries a weight of human challenge. If I really hope then I long for something that is not visible now but is coming. Remember Balaam and his ass: 'I see him – but not in the present, I behold him – but not close at hand' (Numbers 24:17). We know what we want but don't yet see the way to get there. Hope is most prominent in the accounts we read of people in concentration camps and gulags whose quiet dignity in the face of appalling deprivations is an awesome testimony to the human spirit. But it is also present in the men and women in our country who struggle each day for their families despite terrible obstacles.

Finding hope can be hard, but, like Mandela, we must never give up. Though the body may feel limp under the strain, the spirit never gives up its vision of a better way to live. And so besides being an attitude of mind, hope means planning and action. Those who have no hope don't plan. The plans we make and the things we do may be small – like a seed. But we know what seeds do. The source we have in our life in the spirit for this attitude is very powerful. The early church thought that Jesus would return 'soon' but he didn't. What they got instead was the destruction of Jerusalem and the persecution of Nero and Domitian. They had to think again; to plan for a church without Jesus and his apostles. And they did just that. They wrote a record of Jesus' acts and words and they organized the life of the churches. Their hope sustained them and gave them energy to plan and act. Things haven't changed.

8 December, 2006

72

DO NOT FOLD YOUR ARMS

If the fish in a river
Boiled by the midday sun
Can wait for the coming of evening,
We too can wait
In this wind-frosted land,
The spring will come,
The spring will come.

Njabulo S. Ndebele

I met a man just now who said, 'what can we do? Prices are just going up and up. And we have had no water in Mabvuku for a week. They have no mercy, these people. What can we do?

Can I answer the question? I have no answer that will bring him water to wash in this hot weather.

'They look for rent, these people, and impose water charges. But there is no water. If you try to vote, they steal the votes. If you take to the streets, they will shoot you. What can we do?'

Another man put it this way, '(the President) has made scavengers of us all and stripped these grown men of their dignity as they fight over a worn bike tyre. Reduced us all to desperadoes and thieves. Made us small and bleak and old and tired. Made us lose our love of life itself. Split our families and left my parents impoverished, alone, afraid.' (Peter Godwin, When a Crocodile Eats the Sun, p.246). Godwin's book is a memoir in which he describes how the events of the last seven years have affected his own family. It is a moving account of discovery but the undertow is of bitterness and frustration without answers.

We can wait fishlike. The cool of the evening will surely come. But it is hardly enough. Fish can change nothing. They can only wait, fins folded.

There is a waiting though that I can do. Perhaps it is an attitude? 'God clothes the grass in the field that is there today and gone tomorrow. Will he not much more look after you, you people of little faith? So do not worry' (Matt 6:30). I do not take these words to mean we can fold our arms and wait. Actually 'not to worry' is hard work. It implies a tough attitude towards every situation. I will not give in to this situation – at least, and at first, in my mind.

At least in my mind I do not accept this situation. Someone once wrote, 'walls do not a prison make.' The human mind is greater than the stones and bars and laws and cruelty and indifference we see each day. In Zaire (now the Democratic Republic of Congo-DRC) in the hard times of 1993 they used to say, 'il faut pas croiser les mains.' (Do not fold your arms). Jesus, especially in John's passion account is steady, dignified, clear and comes across as somehow in change, whereas Pilate is squirming around trying to find a face-saving way out. Pilate is not prepared to do the one thing he knows he ought to do. He is torn, worried and afraid.

Fish endure, but humans are called to do more than just endure.

10 February, 2007

73

GO AND TELL THE OTHERS

Recent events claimed our attention more closely than usual. The arrests, the beatings, the deaths and the intimidation have concentrated our minds and drawn international comment and warnings. For a moment there was an upsurge of hope that something would happen that would change the situation. But nothing happened and we are back where we were with more frustration and higher prices.

Some day historians will chart what we are living now and put the pieces together. But for the present we live without seeing where we are going. No one has any kind of plan to lift us out of the deep trouble we are in. Talk is about elections and power, not about harvests and empowerment.

'Tears flood my eyes Night and day, unceasingly, since a crushing blow falls on the daughter of my people, a most grievous injury. If I go into the countryside, there lie men killed by the sword; If I go into the city, I see people sick with hunger; Even prophets and priests plough the land; they are at their wit's end. We were hoping for peace - no good came of it! For the moment of cure - nothing but terror!' (Jeremiah 14:17-19)

God's reply to the prophet is not very encouraging. There will be no quick end to the people's woes. There is something they have to learn, something that Gandhi called 'the rightness of our actions.' Gandhi was much more interested in India becoming free through the integrity that comes from truth and the courage to act truthfully. He hated any kind of short-cut that involves violence, slogans or a divisive message. He wanted people to see with what the poets call 'rinsed eyes.' Jimmy Carter, the former US president, quoted the prophet Micah in his inaugural speech; 'to act justly, to love tenderly and to walk humbly with my God' (6:8) and he was considered naive and incompetent.

Churchill called Gandhi a 'half-naked fakir' and Jeremiah lamented that he was a 'daily laughing stock' (20:7). Yet these people put out markers for us. There are things each of us can do, ways each of us can live, that can change things. We do not have to just wait.

22 April, 2007.

74

APOLOGISE? WE GAVE THAT UP LONG BACK.

A person from another country tells of how the Electricity Supply Board sent a letter to residents in her locality warning them a week before that there would be a two-hour cut in power on a certain day between stated hours. Even then the people complained, 'how are we to make our morning tea?'

We have different expectations. But it would be nice to have just a word of explanation, a word of warning so that we could plan and maybe a word of apology. When this is suggested the response is, 'you must be crazy; don't you know we've given up apologising long ago.' And, of course, it is true. When did we last hear a convincing explanation of our economic woes? When did we last have a scheduled plan warning us of power cuts on such and such a day for such and such hours? A nation that gives up explaining, abandons apologies, is on a fast track to losing its way completely.

If you ask the question: 'What are our leaders thinking? They are intelligent men and women; they must know what they are doing,' what answer do you hear? 'There is no logic in it any more. People are just scrambling for what they can get for as long as they can get it. Tomorrow has been cancelled. We just live for today.'

Some years ago a boat full of whiskey foundered on the shore of an island off Scotland. All the islanders descended on the wreck and carried off crates of whiskey before the owners could reclaim their cargo. When the police arrived the islanders had hidden away their treasure and claimed ignorance and innocence and soon a book celebrating the event appeared; *Whiskey Galore*. At times it seems as though our leaders rejoice in power for its own sake; they have found of making fortunes for themselves and they are intent on enjoying that fortune for as long as it will last.

But it seems unbelievably irresponsible to build on sand and just wile away the time while the 'whiskey' lasts. People are dying for lack of medical treatment and now we hear that the UN says crop failures in the southern provinces of Zimbabwe and the rapid erosion of incomes caused by Zimbabwe's annual inflation rate means that about '2.1 million people will face serious food shortages as early as the third quarter of 2007. The number of people at risk will peak at 4.1 million in the first three months of 2008 – more than a third of Zimbabwe's estimated population of 11.8 million.'

7 June, 2007

75

SETTLE WHILE STILL ON THE WAY

As Luke's gospel progresses he gets more and more insistent that a time of crisis is coming and that it is essential to do something before it is too late. He has a parable about a rich man and a poor man and a post-mortem conversation between the former and Abraham. The rich man pleads with Abraham to send the poor man to warn his family but Abraham says it is too late. 'Between us and you a great gulf has been fixed' (Luke 16:26).

But building up to this climax there is still time. A little earlier in the gospel Jesus is astonished, 'how is it you do not know how to interpret these times? ... try to settle [issues while] you are still on the way, (12:56-58).

We are so used to saying, 'let's hope for the best!' 'Let's see what will happen!' We are constantly warned these days – with regard to climate change for example - that this is just not good enough. We have to act now. It will soon be too late. Yet constantly we see that the most intelligent, the most powerful, the richest people on earth are sitting on their hands, putting off the day of decision.

There are many political and practical examples of this attitude in Africa. To take just one far from home and therefore as objective as can be: relations between Eritrea and Ethiopia in the 1940s and '50s were cooperative and friendly. Ominous signs of tension began to appear in the 1960s but no action was taken. Eventually the most terrible war and famine came and the consequences of inaction are still with us. All of this happened because the powerful people did not act wisely when there was still time.

If we look into our mirrors in Zimbabwe today we can see the whole sorry process repeated here. We have had ample time to build relationships between people and to lay the foundations of a good economy that could benefit everyone. We had the resources to build infrastructure for power, water, sanitation and transport, to say nothing of food, medicine and education. And what have we done? We have pursued other goals and just hoped for the best.

If history teaches us anything it tells us this attitude just won't work. It is time to wake up and become engaged in settling the issues before us while we are still 'on the way.' Otherwise it will be too late.

27 October, 2007

76

A LOOK CAN HEAL

In Burma the authorities are refusing to allow aid in to help the victims of a cyclone as they fear aid workers, while helping the people, will learn too much and say too much about the real situation in the country. The rulers' fear of their own position being undermined is greater than their desire to save the lives of their own people. So they are willing to allow many people to suffer or even die so that they remain in power.

What is it that makes human beings so cruel to each other, whether it be Burma or Zimbabwe? It is not a lack of education. Many of the perpetrators have been through schools and higher places of learning. Yet their actions are contrary to reason and common sense. We are supposed to learn how to think at school. But these cruel people do not seem to think either of the effect of their actions on their own families, their own fellow citizens or their place in history. Does it not worry them that, when school teachers in the future are looking for examples of heinous crimes in history, their names will come up? It does not seem to. So education and reason are out as explanations.

What is it then that is behind the unbelievable cruelty we hear about every day in far away countries but also in our own? How does a cruel regime come to implant itself and grab the initiative in a country in such a way that no one can resist? Germany is one country, which suffered this terrible experience under the Nazis. South Africa was another under the Nationalists. An ideology comes to the fore, which has its attractions for some of the people. The majority do nothing but 'wait and hope for the best.' In the meantime the minority take a firm grip on the levers of power and press heavily so that the whole country is forced to follow.

What we are living in Zimbabwe today is a bitter struggle between those who will do anything to hold on to power, even if the country is reduced to penury as a result, and those who sense that people are aching for normality, peace and progress. This struggle has been lived in different ways by many countries. It is a moral struggle in the sense that each person has to decide to become engaged. We cannot say, 'let us wait and see what happens.' If we continue to wait and see we may be condemning ourselves to another twenty years of poverty and want. We don't want another Kenya, far less another Rwanda. It is time to face the one who oppresses. He or she may not even want to be an oppressor. They too may be looking for a way out. There is a story in Luke's gospel (Ch. 19) where an oppressor of the people wanted to see Jesus out of curiosity. He did not want to get involved with him personally. He was short and had to climb a tree to see him. Jesus knew he was an oppressor but he also knew his pain. We are told he just looked at him and invited him to come down from his tree. And we are further told that this simple look opened the floodgates of relief and joy and changed the man's life.

The men who oppress in our society today are ordinary people with families, with difficulties and with hopes. We cannot just condemn them all as evil. Most are crying out for some kind of release from the bonds that tie them. I once saw two photos of the same East German border guards at the time of the Berlin wall. In the first they both looked grim and forbidding. In the second they were smiling and welcoming. The caption underneath read. HOW THEY ARE DEPENDS ALSO ON US.

11 May, 2008

77

LET CONSCIENCE BE MY GUIDE

'If we rigged the elections I could not live with my conscience.' So spoke Robert Mugabe on the day of the elections, 29 March. One might comment that he seems to have had little difficulty living with his conscience since that date while vigorously engineering the result he wants in the run-off in late June. However, the question of conscience remains a pivotal issue in a society like ours where people trample on their conscience with ease. How else can you explain the way soldiers and police 'bash' ordinary citizens who try to exercise the choice they won in the bitter struggle of the 1970s?

Conscience competes in modern society generally with what we call personal autonomy. In fact it has, in the words of a commentator in the *Tablet*, a British Catholic weekly, 'been almost completely eclipsed by belief' in this autonomy. In other words, people do not dig very far within themselves to discover what is right and what is wrong. They get stuck at the point of asking 'what is good for *me* now?' They do not consider what the implications of this action will be for them in the future or what effects it will have on their family, let alone their country. So we choose short-term solutions, which bring instant gratification but which in the long term bring dire consequences.

There is a scene in the play about Sir Thomas More, Chancellor of England, who was sent to the scaffold because of his conscience in the reign of King Henry VIII. The prosecutor in his trial is shown trying to bully a witness into perjury; making him swear he had seen Sir Thomas do something that he clearly had not done. The witness resists for some time but then gives in to the pressure and the enticements and the prosecutor says, 'there, that wasn't too difficult was it? It will be easier next time.' And it is easier next time. Once we begin to silence our conscience and ignore it, it becomes habitual. We have people in our country who have so suppressed their conscience that they act as though they do not have one at all.

What our troubled time (since say 2000) has bequeathed to us is a silenced collective conscience, where corruption, cruelty and greed have taken over from personal responsibility for moral decisions. To return to the *Tablet* commentator, 'the question we never quite answer, week after week, is how do we, as human beings and members of society, reach moral decisions?' It is a question for us today in Zimbabwe. Until we can answer it with some confidence we are likely to continue, no matter who is in government, with unease.

30 May, 2008

78

BREAKING DOWN BARRIERS

The time after the elections was also the time after Easter and there was a daily refrain in the church's readings of the Acts of the Apostles and the Last Supper discourse in John, like the right hand and left hand of a pianist. John gives us the conviction of our oneness in the Father while at the same time Acts records the constant opposition of the Jews to Paul's preaching. They listen to him with initial interest – as for example in Antioch in Pisidia – but once the implications of what he is saying sink in they backtrack and take up a 'no change' position.

It seems the President was true to his words on the day of the voting, saying that 'if we rigged the election I could not live with my conscience.' Two days later he initiated moves to hand over to Morgan Tsvangirai, leader of the opposition party, MDC, but he was quickly reined in by a junta of military leaders and the familiar scenario of propaganda and force was re-oiled and set in motion.

Why do people refuse to do what is obviously right and in their own long-term interest? John raises this question constantly and most dramatically in the story of the man born blind. His only answer is, 'they prefer the darkness'. Ultimately this is the only answer we can give to the present situation in Zimbabwe. But the gospels teem with instances of Jesus breaking through this barrier of evil.

It is frustrating when people simply describe what is happening; someone is beaten, a house is burnt, a sick person dies waiting for attention, a child cannot go to school, but our repeated descriptions do not lead anywhere. Perhaps a few more broken windows; a few more broken bones. And the result? More frustration and weariness. So people choose to endure their suffering and humiliation patiently, day after day, month after month, year after year.

What will happen this month in the run-off? Could we be in for a surprise? Only if we raise our minds out of the dark pit we have dug for ourselves. Some people, after all, did listen to Paul and managed to break through the mindset of their generation. Despite the despair we often feel, with faith, we can break through the impasse in which we find ourselves. We do not have to passively 'wait and see.'

What I am trying to say is well illustrated by the French author, Antoine de St Exupery:

> *When you want to build a ship do not call people with your drum to bring wood and prepare tools; do not give jobs and assign tasks, but awaken in them the yearning for the boundless wide sea.*

In 1980 we were 'free' at last but we were not awake. The 1980s was a passive decade in which people 'enjoyed' the 'fruits' of independence; schools, clinics, services. Today we have, in some way, lost that freedom but now people are awake. Perhaps we are at last ready for a transformation from within, not something coming from outside. Change from outside is ephemeral if it is not built on change from within.

Just this week Ian Paisley is retiring from Northern Irish politics after fifty years in which he moved from bigoted anti-nationalism to tolerance and respect for those who had a different agenda. The *Tablet* describes the developments in Ireland as 'little short of sensational.' What can happen in one part of the world can happen in another.

7 June, 2008

79

YES, WE CAN

A re we learning from this long trauma? Each day we see signs not just of the collapse of structures in our society but also observe our morality seeping away with the cholera bearing effluent in our townships. There are reports of severe food shortages in prisons and people dying. Yet the authorities do not take action. They do not appeal to those who can help because such an action would be an admission of failure, so they let people die.

Dietrich Bonhoeffer, a Lutheran pastor, came to realise the horror of Hitler's regime at a time when most Germans failed to see, let alone to resist, that horror. From his prison cell in 1942 he wrote:

> *There remains an experience of incomparable value.*
> *We have for once learnt to see the great events of*
> *world history from below, from the perspective of the*
> *outcast, the suspects, the maltreated, the powerless, the*
> *oppressed, the reviled, – in short, from the perspective*
> *of those who suffer ... we have to learn that personal*
> *suffering is a more effective key, a more rewarding*
> *principle for exploring the world in thought and action*
> *than personal good fortune.*

Until we begin to understand events 'from below,' we will continue to stifle the little voice within us that questions our lack of courage. If you ask 'what can we do?', you will be told 'it is not our concern.' But what is my concern? Will my grandchildren ask me one day, 'what did you do in those bad days at the beginning of the century?' And I will have to say, 'there was nothing I could do.' 'But, granddad, there were people dying not far from here.'

'The more a person has given to him or her the more will be expected.' It is true that the ordinary person struggling to find food for her family each day can hardly be held responsible for the death of people she does not know. But there are others who know: could we not influence them?

Citizens' rights are usually not eroded in a day. We should never cease to remind ourselves that our present problems go back well before 1980. They started when the first decision was made to restrict the freedoms of the conquered people of this land. Once that foundation stone was laid it was only a matter of building on it, brick by brick, so that by the 1960s Federal Chief Justice Tredgold described our system of laws as 'remov(ing) the last vestige of doubt about whether Southern Rhodesia is a police state.'

When the present government came into power in 1980 it found these laws in place. People were accustomed to them and the new government decided that it too could use them. So all they did was change the colour of the hands on the levers of repression. They wanted to control people and found the tools of control ready to hand. And we, the povo, let it happen. It was not our responsibility. They were the government and we were content to allow them to do what they wanted. We woke from our political slumber in the late 1990s but by then it was too late.

It is encouraging today that everywhere on our continent we see signs of people questioning the system by which governments come to power and stay in power. There has been much excitement this week on seeing one man succeed in overthrowing centuries of prejudice with three words – 'yes, we can' – and in seeing another graciously concede defeat without bitterness or accusations of rigging. We too are on an unstoppable journey. But it does mean somewhere along the line our saying, 'this is my concern.'

7 November, 2008

80

AN END TO VICIOUSNESS

Would that it were so! The decision over the week-end of
the MDC to go into the government was greeted with
enthusiasm by some and with considerable reserve by others. Yet
in such a drawn out crisis where people are at the end of their
wits as to how to survive, the decision of the leader of the MDC
has generally brought widespread hope. People are saying; 'it is
worth a try.' And one word keeps popping up; it is not a solution
but a 'process.' As the MDC people begin to work with the ZANU-
PF people they will both begin to discover the common ground
– something they could never do when one was outside and the
other in.

So the hope is that as the two rub shoulders they will discover
their need for each other in the short term, and in the long term
a solution will only come if there is this opportunity for give and
take in the transition period. The old man is said to be tired and
wanting a way out of the dilemma. So it is a time for magnanimity,
large-heartedness and reconciliation. Zimbabwe may yet be an
example of peacemaking among rivals that will inspire the rest of
the African continent.

But what we can all agree on is that the next weeks and
months are going to be difficult. People who loathe each other
are going to have to learn to work together. In their hearts that
want revenge but in their minds they know this is only stirring
up more hatred and bloodshed. It is going to be very hard to

swallow the things that have happened these past nine years and move on but this is what will be needed. To swallow does not mean to forget. We will need some exercise like the South African Truth and Reconciliation Commission at some point. The TRC, as you remember, worked – not through forgetting all the cruel events of the apartheid years – but by bringing them to light and then moving towards reconciliation. To swallow means to put to one side bitter feelings for the moment and become engaged in the urgent tasks of rebuilding. At a later stage when there is some calm and security, then the pain of the past can be brought into the open so that it may be healed and the nation may fully recover. This exercise will, as so many people say, have to cover not only the recent events of the new century but it will have to reach back to the 1980s if it is to be effective.

Finally it is worth recalling that it is not only a country that grows through a process. Our understanding of reconciliation itself grows. There are passages in the bible full of the desire for violent revenge – Psalm 109, for example. But we are not stuck in these thoughts. By the time we reach the New Testament the message is reconciliation, forgiveness seventy times seven, and loving your enemies.

2 February, 2009

81

I DON'T WANT REVENGE

There is a moving moment in Peter's confident address to the people after he has healed a lame man. He is reminding them about how they handed Jesus over and betrayed him to Pilate and then he says; 'now I know brothers that neither you nor your leaders had any idea what you were really doing' (Acts 3:17). These words came to me when I read recently a Sapa report by Jan Raath about the violence carried out last year when many thousands were tortured and 200 were killed, and how there are now the slow beginnings of a healing process.

A victim who 'had to sleep on his stomach for weeks to allow his wounds to heal (and who) cannot walk much further than a few hundred metres without enduring excruciating pain' wants justice done but not revenge. The report tells us that reconciliation between this victim and his torturer 'took place earlier this year after the Catholic Church's Commission for Justice and Peace took the first steps toward trying to heal the deep psychological and spiritual trauma inflicted in the murderous three-month election campaign.' The CCJP gathered 16 victims to listen, talk and share experiences and then they persuaded seven perpetrators to attend separate sessions though only two admitted their involvement. As one of them spoke he 'was sweating and shaking uncontrollably as he talked of his brutality,' said the co-ordinator. 'He told us tht what he did was evil, that he caused death, and people to suffer. He wanted to look in the eyes of his neighbours, to go back and talk it out.'

[Through these workshops,] 'we saw that we were reopening their wounds for months after they had [been] brutalised. We heard them, and then left ... leaving them in their pain. Victims need not just blankets and food, they need spiritual healing as well.' Perhaps the most important factor was 'the loss of human dignity, and their sense of worthlessness' after their ordeals.[1]

Can it really be that the perpetrators 'had no idea what they were really doing'? When you think of Auschwitz and Rwanda and the many times when people have acted inhumanly to one another you really wonder. The sickening numbing violence that is perpetrated on people – do people honestly not know what they are doing? And yet in the report above the few that have agreed to speak about what they have done are appalled by their own actions. They live in terror. But they have taken the first steps towards healing. One can already sense the size of the task ahead. Healing and forgiveness is possible so long as the person really wants it and is prepared to admit, confess what he or she has done. One of the last words of Jesus as he hung on the cross was, 'Father forgive them; for they do not know what they do.' (Luke 23:34)

Independence Day, 2009

---

1 *Mission Possible, Opening Minds for Meaningful Reconciliation*, Catholic Commission for Justice and Peace, 2010.

82

THINKING OUTSIDE THE BOX

I met a Malaysian the other day and I said to him, 'you were colonised, we were colonised. How come you are where you are and we are where we are?' Malaysia is one of the fastest growing economies of South East Asia. He thought for a moment and replied, 'I've been in Zimbabwe three years and my impression is that Zimbabweans don't think outside the box.'

In these Easter days, some of us may be reading the Acts of the Apostles. There is an extraordinary incident in Chapter 15: we are simply told 'the apostles and elders met to look into the matter.' What was the matter? It concerned a threat to the whole understanding a good Jew would have about his culture and tradition. For centuries this tradition laid down certain laws about circumcision and different foods, etc. If you did not keep these traditions you were not a proper Jew. You had lost your identity. So there was a strong move in the early church – all the early Christians were Jews – to maintain all these practices while at the same time embracing Christianity. Paul was the troublemaker. He was starting to baptise 'pagans' and telling them they did not have to abide by all these traditional Jewish customs.

The more conventional among the early Christians had a hard time with this. He was thinking 'outside the box'. He was proposing a way outside the one they were brought up with and which somehow was tied up with Jewish identity.

The attitude of SADC to one of their own is an example of people failing to think 'outside the box'. But even within our borders, we have so many cases of how we cannot think differently from what is traditional. Without taking to the streets why can't we find ways of doing things differently? There are all sorts of examples in hospitals and schools, on our roads and in our towns of things we just accept and say, 'there's nothing we can do.' We wait for 'traditional' solutions – the ones that worked before. But they don't work now. So we put up with long grass growing along the side of our roads, which reduces visibility and causes accidents – not to mention the potholes and decaying verges. Month after month, we tolerate heaps of rubbish in our towns. We shrug our shoulders when children cannot go to school and sit at home, and patients go to hospitals as a last resort. There are many other things in economic and political life with which we put up because they are 'traditional'. For how long will we say 'there's nothing I can do'?

Isn't it time to 'look into the matter,' to realise that we have autonomy and were not given a mind and a conscience to let it sit dormant?

14 May, 2009

3

HOPE IN SOLIDARITY

83

STAND UP!

Nelson Mandela was a boxer in his youth. When I read this in his autobiography *Long Walk to Freedom*[1] my first reaction was how unseemly for the gracious statesman he became to have been a pugilist in his young days! But, of course, he was a fighter all his life. He engaged with the great issue of his day, constantly shifting his ground, dreaming up new punches. In the end he was floored for 27 years – the longest knockout in history? But we now know it was no knockout at all.

The recent elections in Zimbabwe have left people stunned. Despite the ominous prognosis long before they were held, people clung to a faint hope that they would be a way out of the political morass. In the end these hopes proved illusionary. But what

---

1 Published by Little Brown, New York, 1995.

has depressed people far more is the awareness that there is no leadership engaged in addressing this numbing reality. The 'loyal opposition,' to use a phrase coined from British parliamentary history, are down and out. They fought a good fight – the best they could do in the circumstances. I do not know what else they could have done or could still do. But the bottom line, as Anastasio Somoza said in the context of Nicaragua, the opposition may have won the election but the government won the count.

The question people are asking now is, 'what next?' It is hardly inspiring to say, 'wait for the next round.' People are getting impatient for a solution. They have already suffered for a long time and there is a danger of deepening political polarisation. Something has to be done. Some imaginative thinking is called for, some careful analysis and some risking of comfort.

Just imagine, for example, if everyone was more assertive! What if instead of waiting for hours in queues, as we do, we were to demand service, peacefully but firmly. What if we were to stand up and say, 'I'm a citizen and I want this service?' And what if others were touched by our courage and also stood up to be counted.

One of the most moving scenes in the New Testament is of Peter in Acts. Here was a man who followed Jesus when the going was good, the crowds abounded and he was a chef by association. But this same Peter misunderstood the mission of the Messiah and earned the stinging rebuke – 'get behind me Satan,' (Matt 16:22). And when the crisis came he broke down under the repeated taunts of being 'one of them' saying 'I know not this man of whom ye speak'. (Mark 14: 69-71). Fear, anger, at being identified with someone the crowd called a traitor. Does that sound familiar?

Yet in the Acts of the Apostles Peter, we are told, 'stood up' (Acts 2: 14) and addressed the people in a loud voice. The word for 'stood up' in the Greek is the same word as used to describe the resurrection of Jesus. We are in the time of Easter.

10 April, 2005

84

I AM RESPONSIBLE

I asked a man just back from Ghana, 'how's their constitution?' 'Biased,' he said. I asked another who lives in Zambia. 'It's a struggle.'

Why is accountability such a threat? You'd imagine being accountable would be one way of getting a job done better. A report in the paper tells us the government has built houses in Bulawayo under Operation Garikai. They were however, advised to service the area first with water and a sewer system. But they simply went ahead anyway. The mayor commented that they did not take heed of the Council's warning, and they are left with two options – either government blasts the rocks and destroys the houses or they raze the houses and start afresh.

It is the people's taxes that have been used in this careless manner and no one is answerable. No one will get the sack. Questions and complaints go nowhere. And so we continue. Lack of accountability is contagious. Even in Borrowdale, a smart area of Harare, you can see heaps of uncollected garbage by the gates of protected housing estates. On New Year's day a paper reported a store owner as saying, 'things have never been this bad before' and yet the same article makes the point that there has been 'no political fallout' for the President. In other words the government has inured itself against accountability and we are all getting used to it. It is the way they want it and we all comply.

To insist on accountability in a climate where it does not exist, is difficult. You may find yourself alone and vulnerable. When people become accessories in their own oppression, and when opposition politicians bicker among themselves rather than face the issues of the day, we are on the short road to tyranny.

To enter a New Year without hope is a soulless experience. Yet we can create our own hope. Hope too is contagious. In our own small way we can make demands of each other to be accountable. It *is* a good habit. It could even be a New Year resolution. If everyone did it, it might even become unstoppable, and the nation would be reborn.

19 January 2006

85

RIPPLES OF HOPE

Recently I met a former resident of Zimbabwe who now lives far away. I could see he had strawberries on the side table but he delayed in setting them before us. 'We have to wait for the postman.' He did not enlarge on this enigmatic explanation but after a little while the postman did arrive with the letters – and a carton of cream. 'The postman brings me odd things from the shops. He always looks in to see how we are, whether there are any letters or not.'

I warmed to this postman who daily went beyond 'the call of duty' to give comfort and joy to an elderly couple. Small gestures can raise the confidence of people. They can ignite a sense of solidarity, to use that Polish word again, a sense of communion with others.

Bobby Kennedy, who was assassinated in 1968 as he campaigned to become President of the United States, once spoke of 'ripples of hope'.

Each time a man stands up for an ideal or acts to improve the lot of others, or strikes out against injustice, he sends forth a tiny ripple of hope, and crossing each other from a million different centres of energy and daring, these ripples build a current that can sweep down the mightiest walls of oppression and resistance.

Few are willing to brave the disapproval of their fellows, the censure of their colleagues, the wrath of society. Moral courage is a rarer commodity than bravery in battle or great intelligence. Yet it is the one essential vital quality for those who seek to change a world that yields most painfully to change. And I believe that in this generation those with the courage to enter the moral conflict will find themselves with companions in every corner of the globe. For the fortunate among us there is the temptation to follow the easy, familiar paths of personal ambition and financial success so grandly spread before those who enjoy the privilege of education. But that is not the road history has marked out for us. Like it or not we live in times of danger and uncertainty. But they are also more open to the creative energies of people than any other in history...

The gospel image for 'this one essential vital quality' is 'salt' (Matt 5:13). It is salt that makes food palatable and nourishing. It also preserves. It gives life. Every culture has sought to secure its supplies of salt. Its link with life itself can be seen in the stories among the Dande people about Guruuswa. The highest compliment you can pay to another person is to call him or her 'the salt of the earth'. We have many amongst us who could be so called but at the moment they are as hidden as the substance itself as it quietly does its work.

25 January, 2006

86

RUSHING TO THE RESCUE

Recently I met someone who was on the spot when a fire destroyed the top floor of Mater Dei Hospital, Bulawayo, on the 26 August last year. An electrical fault is the prime suspect. But it was the outcome not the cause that gives rise to wonder.

Although the fire occurred at 10.00 at night, 21 patients were evacuated safely from the floor and they were even able to take their cell phones with them to call relatives. Just one person died. The fire brigade was quickly on the spot and put out the fire. The patients were gathered on the lawn and all the doctors of Bulawayo came to offer their services. As the word spread it seems the whole of Bulawayo came to see what they could do. Jews, Muslims and people of different religious and political persuasions – all rose above their differences in a moment of crisis. They brought sheets and blankets, made beds and helped clean the debris. By noon the following day all the patients, except one baby, were back in the hospital or in the adjoining convent and were being cared for as before.

Once again, as so often in history, crisis brought people together and pulled down the walls between them. 'He has broken down the barrier which used to keep us apart' (Ephesians 2: 14). The one who shared this account with me was full of praise for everyone in Bulawayo. She feels it is a wonderful city where people are united and have a strong sense of community.

Chinua Achebe, writing about Nigerians says:

> *There is nothing basically wrong with the Nigerian*
> *character. There is nothing wrong with the Nigerian land*
> *or climate or water or air or anything else. The Nigerian*
> *problem is the unwillingness of its leaders to rise to the*
> *responsibility, to the challenge of personal example, which*
> *are the hallmarks of true leadership.*[1]

There is nothing wrong with the people of Bulawayo or Harare or Gutu or anywhere else. Given the opportunity of responding to the crisis in our midst they would all happily rush to the scene and offer whatever help they could. But there is one thing needed: an admission that there is a crisis and a willingness to accept help in resolving it. If we go on saying: 'Crisis! What crisis?' and denying anything is wrong, the flames simply spread.

27 March, 2006

---

1   *The Trouble with Nigeria* by Chinua Achebe. Heinemann Publishers, Oxford. 1984. p.1.

87

AWAKENING

The time for reconstruction is not far away. It is true we are still descending ever deeper into the pit. But the time for climbing out of it is close upon us. Many people are thinking about that and the sort of Zimbabwe we want to create. Among all the ideas that compete for attention the question of property is central. This is the opinion of Craig Richardson in a paper he calls 'Learning from Failure',[1] in which he closely examines what caused the collapse of Zimbabwe.

Many reasons have been put forward, he says, for our descent into poverty: persistent droughts, foreign sanctions, lavish spending on veterans and irresponsible macro-economic policies. But the one that lies as the hidden concrete foundation of the building, that has come crashing down – and which is 'virtually invisible to [the] inhabitants,' is property rights. The argument is simple: if you are not going to own the product of your labour, you are not going to work.

Since 2000 the government of Zimbabwe has persistently destroyed the right to private ownership. Richardson believes that if the example of Nicaragua, where something similar happened, is anything to go by, we are in for a long haul to restore it. He defines secure property rights as promoting (i) trust that my investment will be secure, (ii) 'land equity, which allows wealth

1   'Learning from Failure: Property Rights, Land Reforms and the Hidden Architecture of Capitalism'. 6 April 2006. Available on <https://www.aei.org/publication/learning-from-failure-2/>

in property to be transformed into other assets,' for example, as collateral to secure loans and (iii) incentives. These have been withdrawn and 'watching Zimbabwe's economic unravelling is chillingly reminiscent of watching a building collapse in slow motion after a series of timed explosions.'

The hasty decisions of 2000 have had huge ripple effects far beyond the small white community at whom they were originally directed. In the twentieth century, at a time when ownership was under attack from various manifestations of Marxism, deep reflection repeatedly reaffirmed its importance. Pope John XXIII wrote in 1961, 'history and experience testify that in those political regimes which do not recognize the rights of private ownership of goods, productive included, the exercise of freedom in almost every other direction is suppressed or stifled. This suggests, surely, that the exercise of freedom finds its guarantee and incentive in the right of ownership.'

To affirm that a government should respect property rights is not to say these rights have some absolute value. The common good of all the people requires any government to ensure that some do not become excessively rich while others barely survive in grinding poverty. As many countries have proved, provisions can be made that safeguard the interests of the poor while at the same time respecting the general right to ownership. Incentives are built into the first page of the Bible (Genesis 1:28) and no one gets anywhere without them. They are the foundations we have to restore in our farms and towns.

25 April, 2006

88

HIDE-OUTS

A hideout is where a writer disappears to concentrate undisturbed or a robber finds a place to keep his goods. But recently I heard the word used of a man who works in the informal sector. He had to hide away in order to work. He could find no 'legal' place. If he wanted one, he had to wait while bureaucracy trudged its unhurried way and then he would have to pay. So he prefers to just get on with his work but out of sight. If local government authorities find him he may be reported to the police and have his tools and his wares confiscated. If the Electricity Authority (ZESA) discovers him using a welding machine 'at home' they too may prosecute him.

But if there are hindrances from without there are others from within. People hide their intentions from their work colleagues. There is a huge market for bricks. Our exiles are sending cash home and they want houses built. But in a small brick-making project the workers cannot agree with their managers who want transparent accountancy. 'They are too strict.' In other words the managers want receipts. So the project has come to a halt even though the market, the capital and the resources are there.

Projects fail because we do not think them through and we do not commit ourselves to the process that will make them work. Thorns are still choking us (Matthew 13:7). Zimbabwe itself is a 'project'. It was started with enthusiasm but soon hindrances appeared – from without and within. From outside there was the obvious example of ESAP, which everyone now recognises did more harm than good. But from inside too there are blockages to progress where people want quick results – 'Sweet without sweat.'

For six years or more we have watched the great project decline and we have searched the horizon for signs of change. Have we seen any? Yes. Despite the twisting and turning people do to make the 'economy' work for them; there are signs of planning and working for a better tomorrow. For example, these 'hideout' industries, small as they are, teach people creativity and resilience. If you want to make something work you have to be ingenious. You have to find a way through all the hindrances. Even finding spare parts may be a nightmare. You may not find them here. You may have to head for South Africa. Crossing that border today is a challenge in itself. Everything resists us these days: money, borders, laws, permits, premises, credit, transport – even our own colleagues. Anyone who faces some or all of these is learning a lot along the way. Whether we know it or not we are producing a nation of initiators just waiting to come out of their hideouts.

31 August, 2006

89

'THE ZIMBABWE WE WANT'

This is the title of a document launched by the Churches of Zimbabwe on the 27 October 2006 with the aim of being 'our humble contribution to the search for a solution to the challenges faced by our nation'. It is a provisional work setting out markers towards a shared national vision and is the result of months of reflection by the Evangelical Fellowship, the Council of Churches and the Catholic Church. The word 'churches' – pleasingly and imperceptibly slips into the singular on the very first page, signifying a unity among Christians that the President was quick to notice.

Yes, the President was there and this was puzzling. The event was billed as the launch of a dialogue, and my understanding was that it would be a chance for the church leaders to brief their members about the thinking behind the initiative and procedures proposed to carry it forward. To invite the very person you hope to persuade of your approach before you've agreed a position seems to be like an own goal in the opening moments of play.

Indeed, the President in a diplomatic but still telling way, took the opportunity presented to him to undermine the entire initiative. He first told the church leaders (all men and one women) that they may wear clerical collars but they are subject to the same temptations as anyone else. They have no privileged insight into solutions for the country. He then went on to declare the document 'utopian', as if to say, 'you can come up with beautiful solutions to our problems from your theology and spirituality but we deal in the hard realities of everyday politics.' Finally he rubbished the proposal for a new constitution by sacralising the Lancaster House Constitution. It was born of the blood of those who gave their lives in the struggle and was wrested from a faint-hearted British government. What could be more 'home-grown' than that.

The President cleverly pulled the carpet from under the church leaders and neutralised the meeting before anyone knew what was happening. It became clear the government has no intention to enter into dialogue. So that carefully planned and expensive meeting by the churches ran into the sand.

So, yet again, no progress. But are there any lessons to be learnt? I am reminded of a far more risky meeting in the thirteenth century when Francis, 'God's fool' of Assisi, went to meet the Sultan of Egypt, Malek al-Kamil, at a time when Christians and Muslims were at each other's throats. Malek was astonished by this humble, fearless and joyful man. They achieved. Francis did not believe peace can be 'made'. It must be 'embodied'. In other words techniques and position papers can only work if the people involved are people of peace. This goes very deep.

At the launch referred to above, the All Africa Conference of Churches President, Revd Dr John Gatu, narrated some words of the late John Garang, Sudanese leader of the SPLA. Dr Gatu asked him if one could ever trust an Arab? Garang replied, 'do not ask for trust, but give trust.'

We have not got there yet.

27 October, 2006

90

A NEW YEAR

A nything new gives us a thrill even if it is only for a moment. A new baby, a new home, even a new coat. It suggests freshness, an opening to excitement. It expresses our longing for something beyond what we now experience. Ultimately it contains intimations of the eternal. If we listen to the familiar words of the Christmas texts something may strike anew, like the words, 'there was no room for them at the inn' (Luke 2:7). If we draw on our science as well as our faith we ponder that it took billions of years to reach the moment where the creator was born into his creation. It had even taken thousands of years to prepare human beings for this event. Yet when it actually arrived there was 'no room' for him. People did not want something new; 'the old is good enough,' they said (Luke 5:39).

We celebrated Christmas against the background of national and world events. An Eritrean friend wrote that Somalia moved 'from misery to misery'. No one it seems can move that country to a new level of life. There is 'no room' yet for compassion, healing and community. In Iraq the violence goes on and the former ruler was deliberately and formally killed. What does this act actually achieve? Does it promise any breakthrough into a new level of reconciliation and brotherhood? Or is it just more of the old 'eye for an eye, tooth for a tooth?' There is no room for anything except what we're used to.

In our own country there was a congress in Goromonzi. Did

anything new come from it. Were we inspired with any hope for 2007? Again there was 'no room' for imagination, generosity, big-mindedness, reconciliation. No: just more of the old resentments and justifications.

And there is not much sense of happiness about our new year. People seem only to be grimly determined to keep going, whatever happens. 'What else can we do?' Indeed. Indications about rising prices for everything food, school fees, school uniforms, etc, are very frightening. We've invented euphemisms such as 'top -ups' which really means five times or more of the original fee.

Meanwhile the rains do not come and older people are very aware that the climate is changing. We now know that climate change is 'man made' and is due to our saturating the planet with carbon emissions. But we make 'no room' for obvious solutions.

However despite this 'encircling gloom' there is one factor that is always with us – human resilience. All over the world people do not give up. In the deserts of Somalia and Darfur as well as in the urban deserts of Zimbabwe people keep going, ever resourceful, ever intent on providing for their children. They make room for hope. Each new year is a moment of celebration, a moment that is invested in a different future.

2 January, 2007

91

DAMASCUS

To Christians, the word 'Damascus' has become synonymous with a conversion, a turning point, a sudden insight that changes a life. 'Damascus' now evokes a new experience of understanding that leads to a new beginning. That was the experience of Saul of Tarsus, though far from 'new eyes' he actually went blind for a little while.

Many artists and musicians begin their careers learning from their masters. But there always comes a time when they strike out on their own. A conversion takes place from student or apprentice to fully fledged practitioner – an artist creates something uniquely their own, a novelist publishes a first book, an actor interprets a role that gives the part an added freshness. Sometimes such an evolution or development does not result from a formally learned experience. Gandhi,[1] for example, was thrown out of a 'whites only' carriage onto a barren platform in the middle of a cold South African night. It was an event that changed his life. For Ignatius of Loyola[2] it began with a bullet in

---

1   Mohandas Gandhi was born in 1869 into the Hindu merchant caste family in western India. He trained as a lawyer at the Inner Temple, London, and went to practise in South Africa. There the experience of segregation and discrimination changed his life. He became a powerful advocate of non-violent civil disobedience. Returning to India in 1915, he became one of the most powerful and influential advocates of Indian independence.

2   Born in 1491, Saint Ignatius of Loyola was a Spanish priest and theologian, who founded the religious order called the Society of Jesus and became its first Superior General.

the leg. For Rosa Parks[3] it was refusing to give up her seat on an Alabama bus.

These are well-known conversions. But there are countless others – moments that have changed lives. The secret in life, perhaps, is to long for such moments, to watch for doors opening.

Why is conversion so hard for politicians and men of power. It seems that for them any change is risky. Their whole identity is tied up in wanting to come across as consistent. Of Margaret Thatcher it was said, 'the lady's not for turning'. She would not budge from her policies no matter what the evidence of their effects on the lives of people. There have been exceptions. When the House of Commons pushed through the reform Act of 1867 extending the vote to all adult males, the Prime Minister, Benjamin Disraeli, commented; 'now we will have to educate our masters,' and introduced an Education Bill extending schooling to millions of children. Perhaps that was not conversion but expediency, but at least he had the courage to adopt a new policy.

And what of our own leaders? Is there any sign of conversion. Or is 2007 going to be just more of the same. Conversion is a personal thing – I am the only one I can convert. But I can help create conditions that will open the door to change. I can force no one. But one conversion can send out shock waves. Good example can be powerful and inspiring.

Jesus' first recorded words in the gospels are 'The time has come, and the kingdom of God is close at hand. Be converted, and believe...' (Mark 1:15). If we close our doors and our eyes we may never reach Damascus.

26 January, 2007

---

3   Rosa Parks is a black American who in 1955, at the age of 32, refused to obey a bus driver's order to give up her seat in the coloured section of the bus to a white passenger, after the white section had been filled. She was subsequently arrested for civil disobedience for violating Alabama segregation laws. Today she is known as the 'first lady of civil rights' and the 'mother of the freedom movement'.

92

LET US GO ELSEWHERE

Jesus had a busy day in Capernaum and he rose early the next morning to find a quiet place to pray. The crowds, Simon and his companions told him, were looking for him. But he answered, 'let us go elsewhere'. The crowds, or the disciples, wanted to manage Jesus. They enjoyed the hype surrounding his instant fame. But he knew, from his early morning prayer, that he had to move to other places.

The essence of leadership is to 'go ahead' (John 10:4), to know the way, to go elsewhere. When you think of the cell gate on Robben Island clanging shut on Nelson Mandela in 1964, not to open for 27 years, you are caught up in the awesome mystery of leadership. How does a person have the courage to grasp a moment of history ahead of others and say, 'this is the way'? In 1940, when the British were confused by Hitler's apparently unstoppable march through Europe,[1] some of their leaders wanted to seek an accommodation with him, Churchill put into words a resolve to stand up to him, to show the courage that people longed for, but had all but abandoned.

Unfortunately, history does not abound with examples of great leadership. Far too frequently we meet those who follow rather than lead. They follow the fears of their citizens or their own desire to enjoy power for its own sake. At the memorial

1 In 1938 Hitler invaded Sudetenland and Austria, in 1939 he invaded Poland and Czechoslovakia, in 1940 he invaded Belgium and France, and he was threatening to invade Norway.

service in 1995 for the assassinated Israeli Prime Minister, Yitzhak Rabin, King Hussein of Jordan, deeply moved, spoke of Rabin as a man of courage who moved out of the sterile swamp of Israeli-Palestinian politics to reach for peace among the people of the Middle East.

Are those who lead Zimbabwe today able to lay hold of the deep longings of the people for security, respect, freedom and the basic necessities of life? 'Are they able to go elsewhere?' Are they able to chart a course that will make Zimbabweans say, 'this is what we want and how we want the world to perceive us'?

Or are they resolutely moving in the opposite direction? Every day brings news of new restrictions and controls: bread. cooking oil, sugar and other basics are disappearing from the shops. Transport is no longer on the roads. People take three days to travel from Gweru to Harare and those who grow tomatoes in Mutoko see them rot at the side of the road. And security? There is constant fear of arrest and assault.

Sadly, many Zimbabweans are reacting with their own version of 'let's go elsewhere'. They feel they have to leave for the sake of their families. What we are waiting for is the leaders to say, 'let us do things differently'.

6 September, 2007

93

HOPE

In the days to come
the mountain of the Temple of the Lord
shall tower above the mountains ...

So begins the season of Advent in the enigmatic poetical language of Isaiah, meaningless at first glance but like so much in scripture so suggestive of something new breaking in on the human story. The people brooded over their city destroyed by the Assyrians but Isaiah gives them a message that raises their minds and hearts way beyond the present disaster to a time when 'all the nations will stream to it' (2:1-5). This vision must have seemed sheer nonsense to most of his hearers. Is there any kind of evidence that things are about to change? How can you talk of Jerusalem as the hope of the nations when it has been flattened by the invaders?

Hope is indeed the word synonymous with Advent. We call it a virtue in the sense that it is a wonderful thing to experience – like love. Hope is that quality that looks each day for a breakthrough – not necessarily a big breakthrough (like immediate reconciliation in Zimbabwe) but a breakthrough nonetheless. It is the breakthrough where a husband suddenly sees the gift he has in his own wife and learns to see her through new eyes. It is the breakthrough of a carer who suddenly realises that a person with intellectual disabilities has other wonderful gifts. It is the breakthrough of a friend of mine who had cancer. He hoped and hoped the doctors could do something. But they could not and – irritatingly – they would not tell him they could not. Then he realised himself that he was going to die. He was just 27. In his agony and his prayer he became quiet. He began to accept what was about to happen and he even acquired a new happiness. What a breakthrough!

In genuine hope we do not set the agenda. Our hope is centred not on ourselves and 'what I want' but on the other, whether that be my wife, the one I work with or God. Hope is to raise that centre of my being, that place from which all my longings spring, to a higher level away from myself to the other. We do not set the agenda, neither do we set the pace. How things happen, when they will happen, is unsure. All we do is keep alive that longing, that attentiveness. Jesus calls it 'watching', 'staying awake'. Otherwise, he says, we will be like the people in Noah's day who were eating and drinking, taking wives and husbands ... and the flood came and swept them all away (Matt 24).

So, once again this Advent as in so many Advents in recent years, we in Zimbabwe are invited to hope. It is not a useless exercise, a soporific, a dose of opium. It is a deeply human and noble response to the challenges and horrors we face. A hopeful people is a people alive, awake, attentive and ready.

1 December, 2007

94

BEING READY FOR SURPRISES

Anyone who reads the Advent scriptures might be hard put to enter the minds of John the Baptist's listeners two thousand years ago at the Jordan River. The Jordan itself had deep associations for the people for its crossing was the way they first entered the Promised Land. And further, here was this unusual person dressed in camel hair and eating locusts and wild honey – the very dress and food of Elijah. For them, if not so immediately for us, there was something in the offing. 'All Judea,' we are told, came out to hear him. And he spoke of imminent change. Away with the old securities! Do not think merely saying, 'we have Abraham for our father' will save you on the day of decision. 'The axe is already laid to the roots of the trees' (Matt 3) and judgment is fast approaching. 'His winnowing fan is in his hand; he will clear his threshing floor and gather his wheat into his barn; but the chaff he will burn in a fire that will never go out.'

Fierce language, and language that we have got used to so that it does not startle us as it did the people at the Jordan that day. Yet we are moved by much the same feelings. We search for securities and yet we long for change. We belong to a particular nationality, group or family – even church – and this gives us identity and security. Even our economic or social position may give us electricity and water when others go without these things.

But expectancy? Looking forward to something new: marriage, our first child, a new job and new prospects. And for a people?

As 1979 became 1980, how we looked forward to the new order! Huge changes, huge possibilities were imminent. The excitement was everywhere: buses going to Highfield to greet the leaders returning from the bush were filled with people longing for a new start, confident and proud.

Where are those dreams now? Well, they are not gone. They are just more realistic. Anticipation is more rooted in what really might be possible. Sometimes we are caught off guard by good news: did you know, for instance, that between the early 1980s and 2001 global 'poverty rates fell by almost half: approximately 400 million people crossed the US $1 a day (a measure of extreme poverty) threshold during this time. This amounts to a fairly dramatic reduction in poverty globally. There is thus no basis for views, often expressed by protesters against globalisation and privatisation, that these trends have coincided with a rise in global poverty'.[1] The improvement took place in Asia, especially China, and hardly touched Africa. Health services and education remain key factors in the battle against poverty. We prided ourselves on the strides we made in these areas in the 1980s but now we know they were not priorities and schools today are bleeding from the flight of teachers.

At any rate, this is the season of anticipation and we should be ready for good news any time.

5 December, 2006

---

1   *Understanding Poverty* by A. V, Banerjee, R. Benabou and D. Mookherjee. Oxford University Press, Oxford, 2006.

95

LIVING IN A DIFFERENT WAY

Dorothy Day ran a house in New York for people who were down and out and at the same time she wrote and spoke about justice, 'God meant things to be much easier than we have made them,' she said. Christmas is racing towards us again. Do we have the time to ponder its meaning? Harry Belafonte used to sing, 'man will live for ever more because of Christmas Day' in a haunting way. Do we have a sense that behind all the wrapping paper our world has been changed utterly by that event in Bethlehem? Do we have the time to extend our personal understanding of our faith to take in the extraordinary nature of what happened?

'God became flesh'. Words simply stated, but so extraordinary that people have ever since wanted to share their understanding of them with others. Those fragile ships brought colonisers as well as preachers of the gospel. The former often used force and had their eyes on trade and profit. The latter, on the whole, used persuasion and focused on assisting the people they worked among. I happened to be at the Cape of Good Hope recently and I found it exhilarating to look out to sea and imagine those fragile sailing ships turning this corner five hundred years ago and carrying men like Francis Xavier to India, Indonesia, Japan and the shores of China at a time when people in the rest of the world hardly knew such places existed. People gave their whole lives and even went to their deaths to witness to that Bethlehem event. Those who took time to ponder understood what St John meant when he wrote, God loved the world so much that he gave everything to save it from ruin.

The message is clear: live in such a way that the earth yields its gifts to all people and not just to some. Everything has been given to us so that *all* people can live and grow in peace and find *all* that they need on this earth. As it is, the greed of some has barred the way for the needs of many to be satisfied.

At this moment in South Africa there is a large ANC meeting about personalities and policies. Essentially they are asking the same question. Will South Africans be able to find a way for the many to enjoy a way of life, which at present is only enjoyed by a few? It is a huge challenge, a call made all that time ago in Bethlehem; 'peace to people of good will' (Luke 2:14).

There is a lot of good will around. People want to work and they want to help improve the lives of others. But they are not pushing on open doors. As 2008 approaches we may be inclined to have more dread than hope. There is nothing to suggest it will be an easier year than 2007. Yet the ancient yet ever new message of Bethlehem can sustain us and help us to live differently so that life will become easier for all.

17 December, 2007

96

THIS IS IT

We all have moments when we say, 'this is it', the moment I've been looking forward to or the moment I've been dreading. A footballer from Africa is signed up with a European club and all eyes are on him as he makes his way on to the field for the first time. This is it. This is a moment when my life is going to change and I'm a bit scared about what it might mean. I both want it and don't want it. We so rarely know precisely what the future holds in store for us.

Or perhaps the turning point is the result of a disaster. A sudden illness or the collapse of a project. A woman discovers her status: she is positive and she knows it's not her fault. She has dreaded this moment and now it has happened. Or a man invests all he has in a new farm and there is drought and he gains nothing. This is it. It's a catastrophe, but also a defining moment.

How do we react? There is a scene in the film *Zorba the Greek* where the hero sees all his efforts come crashing down. He has designed a procedure to transport timber from the mountain down to the sea by a cable held up by pylons. The first log comes down successfully but the second one sets up a vibration that increases from pylon to pylon until the whole system collapses. What does Zorba do? Does he swear and blame the workmen? Does he blame God or the government? No, he dances on the beach.

This week we have elections in Zimbabwe. This is it! There is no consensus about what will happen. Everyone has his or her own prophecy. We will know soon which was right. But there is no uncertainty about the fact that we have longed for this moment – and also dreaded it.

I write these words on Good Friday. Jesus approached this day with a sense of 'this is it'. He longed for that day – and dreaded it. 'He resolutely took the road for Jerusalem' knowing full well what would happen there (Luke 9:51). But when he got there he prayed, 'Father save me from this hour' (John 12:27). The mixture of longing and dread underlies a very human experience. New life, growth, salvation, does not come without a price.

So, this is it. It is not a 'normal' election. It is filled with uncertainties. It could be a disaster. It could be a triumph. It could be a moment of liberation, going deeper than the experience of 1980. What it will be depends also on us.

21 March, 2008

97

THE ONE AND THE MANY

What difference will my vote make? Or, since you are reading this after the elections, what difference has it made? People have wondered from ancient times about the relationship of the individual to the whole group. Some Greek philosophers argued that the group is made up of individuals and therefore the individual is more fundamental, while others said the group is what gives the individual his or her identity and so it was more important. Is Tonderai Moyo more important than Zimbabwe or is Zimbabwe more important than Tonderai? This debate may sound like an academic tussle with little relevance to us in April, 2008. But the question remains: do our individual choices really affect the destiny of the whole?

As I write, I, like everyone else, have no idea what is going to happen over the next few days. Are people going to see their individual votes have a collective effect in deciding who our rulers will be? Or are they going to have their individual choices crushed by some behemoth they cannot resist? Prayers have risen all over the Republic for peaceful fruitful elections but these prayers depend on a collective desire for what is asked for.

One thing is certain. Individuals in this country are far more conscious, than they were in 1980, of what they want. They know they inhabit a country rich in talent and resources. All that is needed is proper management. This has been denied them for too long and people are utterly tired of the frustration they are now enduring. The question is whether they can translate that frustration into votes that count.

Another thing is certain. Everywhere in Africa there is movement towards accountability in elections. President Kaunda of Zambia was hailed as some kind of hero in 1991 when he respected the will of the people and resigned from office after losing the election. Ever since, in Zambia and elsewhere, there has been a demand for accountability and, even if it has not always been listened to, the pressure is on. Every election gets more fiercely contested. One of our most fervent prayers is that this contest remains peaceful and non-violent. The recent Kenyan elections cast a long dark shadow over Africa.[2] It is tragic that so many were so cruelly killed or driven from their homes. But it does mean that never again in Kenya will anyone be able to flout the will of the voters.

We are in Easter time as the early days of April are upon us. There cannot be a man or woman among us who is not hoping for a release from the knots we have tied ourselves in these past ten years. Our hope is not unfounded. It is based on painful experience and the good news of Easter.

28 March, 2008

---

2   Following the elections in December 2007, hundreds of thousands of people were displaced from their homes, and more than a thousand died in the post-election violence. Many members of large ethnic groups attacked anyone whom they felt didn't belong; minorities and people that had come from other countries were common targets. For a few weeks, anarchy prevailed with rioting, looting, and the breakdown of law and order.

98

WAITING

As the poet says, 'they also serve who only stand and wait'.[3] We have done a lot of waiting. We are now into the fifth day. It is becoming clear that this patient waiting is a powerful response. The international media has asked hundreds of questions, all demanding answers. Meanwhile the people wait. I was out of town on Monday and when I returned I searched the faces of people as I came through the city to see if I could detect any news. Nothing! They were just going about the business of getting home.

Meanwhile there have been rumours – plenty of them. When there are no facts people feed on rumours. If something did not actually happen, well, it could have. There was the rumour that the government wanted to provoke a situation where they could declare a state of emergency. But wiser councils, so the rumour goes, prevailed: people would not allow themselves to be provoked. Instead they would wait – and they do. Perhaps in another country people would have exploded by now. But we haven't. And we won't. People have different virtues. Zimbabweans have patience. You can throw anything at them. They will not react. You can take away their farms, bulldoze their houses and destroy their livelihoods and still they will wait.

---

3   John Milton 1608-74 was an English poet, polemicist, man of letters, and dedicated civil servant for the Commonwealth of England under Oliver Cromwell. He became blind, and wrote a poem 'On his Blindness' which contain this last line: 'they also serve who only stand and wait'.

'You are the ones who have stood by me faithfully in my trials,' (Luke 22:28). Actually, the apostles didn't. They denied they knew Jesus and ran away. But despite their failures their hearts were with him and they eventually came together and huddled in a safe house waiting for something to happen. Perhaps I should wait before completing these few words and see what happens...

It is now the seventh day and we are still waiting. The news is that the government wants a recount. This implies they know what they want to recount. But the rest of us don't. Hopes have risen and fallen all week. Underneath it all people are waiting – and maybe growing stronger. This happens when passive patience moves to active patience: when just saying 'there is nothing we can do' moves to an active alert attention to everything and looks for opportunities to make a difference. In a word, when hope drives out fear.

6 April, 2008

99

WE CAN ALL BE MONSTERS

M ost of us have short memories. But those who suffer deeply don't forget. How many of us remember that only last year in July we heard that aid workers were warning us of the first signs of looming famine and that a third of the population was chronically malnourished? Attempts to assist them were blocked by a ban on foreign agencies working in rural areas after the government said they were fronts for 'regime change' by Britain and the United States. Do we also remember that in November there were reports of sewage flowing in the streets, endless mounds of rubbish, broken water pipes and an imminent cholera epidemic that had the Health Minister admitting he was scared. These were social realities we endured in the past twelve months quite apart from all the dramatic political movements.

We may be already forgetting but the people who were in charge then are still in charge. Those who have come into government since are struggling daily to address the urgent issues before us, but they are handicapped by opposition from the very people they are working with. It is an extraordinary situation. But they are keeping cool. No one is raising his or her voice and blaming others. It is as though they recognise the unique situation and that it will only be a series of small victories where everyone is a winner that will eventually resolve the situation.

Ingrid Betancourt, the most high-profile captive of the Colombian rebels, was asked after her rescue in 2008 why she does not denounce the crimes committed by her guards. She replied, 'if I do bear witness one day it will have to be to teach people something. I want people to understand that we all, deep down inside us, can be monsters.' Her questioner persisted, 'even you?'

'Yes,' she went on, 'of course. You can find someone nice and kind and fun to talk to and then, because of an order or an ideology, they become an executioner. There are lots of ways of crushing others in everyday life. When someone speaks to you and you don't answer them, that is aggression, you are humiliating them. When someone asks for help and you lie to get out of it, you're denying their right to ask for help.'

Our present experience is calling us to rise above selfish concerns and look to the good of everyone; to work imaginatively and patiently for reconciliation. It does not mean forgetting what happened but it does mean grasping the present opportunity to build something new. And that, of course, is what Easter is about.

14 April , 2008

100

SEEKING AND SEEING

There is a village seven miles from Jerusalem and two of Jesus' friends, fed up with waiting for something to happen, decided to go there. On their way Jesus himself sought them out and 'walked by their side'. The late Jacques Dupuis, a Belgian priest, who ran into difficulty with the Vatican over his views on dialogue between religions, once said 'salvation history does not start with Abraham. It starts with creation. Throughout human history God has been seeking the human beings he created.' God is seeking us, looking for us.

The search takes many different forms and we know them by the way we label them. We may see it as we doing the searching but it is really God who sees us while we are 'still a long way off' (Luke 15:20). The labels we are familiar with are the Christian churches with their different names; Islam with its different forms; Hinduism; Buddhism; and so forth. These are the ways in which people have been drawn to God by holy men and women.

But there are other ways of searching whose labels are outside of the religions of the world. Literature, music and art in all its forms are ways in which people have tried to reach out to truth and in so doing have, like the desperate woman in the gospel (Mark 5:28), 'touched his clothes'. And going further, every act of making or doing, or of relating to others is either a response to the One who searches or is a turning away.

What is the outcome then of this quest in its many forms? It is to see and know. Over a hundred years ago the painter, Paul Cezanne, painted the mountain near his home in Southern France, Mont St Victoire, countless times in an endless search to 'see' it and to express on canvas what he saw. His paintings now sell for millions of US dollars because people recognise that his works lead us beyond our daily experience to something that is inexpressible.

But again it is not just holy men and artists who map the way for us. Every act of 'seeing' can be a response to God's search for us. The poet, John O'Donohue, has a poem for the mother of a young criminal:

> *No one else can see beauty in his darkened life now.*
> *His image has closed*
> *Like a shadow.*
> *But he is yours:*
> *and you have different eyes*
> *that hold his yesterdays*
> *in pictures no one else remembers.*
> *He is yours in a way no words could ever tell;*
> *And you can see through the stranger this deed has made him*
> *And still find the countenance of your son.*

Jesus's two friends did not recognise him because they had grown used to only partly seeing him. As he continued his search for them, through explaining the scriptures and breaking the bread, they suddenly saw him.

17 April, 2008

101

A TIME FOR BUILDING

The Christian church was reared in a Jewish nest. The most obvious thing for the disciples to do after Jesus ascended to heaven was to be 'continually in the temple' as we are told in the closing words of Luke. They knew themselves as Jews and only gradually, and with much pain, did they realise that 'welcoming Greeks' meant they would have to adapt their Jewish ways to others who came with different experiences. Chapter 15 of Acts tells us what a mighty struggle that was and how the early Christian community had to build something new and neither Jesus nor anyone else told them how to do it. They had to sweat at it themselves.

I recently was able to experience at first hand the toleration and reconciliation that has painfully been achieved in one corner of the world where people had been enemies for centuries. The British colonised Ireland in the twelfth century and it was only in the twentieth that most of the country was able to free itself. The remaining bit, 'the North', clung to the United Kingdom. In the 1960s the civil rights movement in the USA influenced the people of the North who resented British rule to demonstrate peacefully for change. But their protest was met with violence and so they too took to violence and the whole situation spun out of control for 25 years, causing the deaths of hundreds. Huge efforts were made in the late 1990s to construct a peace agreement and what I saw was a community well on the way to reconciliation. People who hated and despised one another are now calmly living side by side, getting to know one another and developing the Province together.

It is challenging for people to move from the security of their identity built up over generations and to respond to the need of a new reality that is breaking in on them. These two examples – one ancient and one modern – show it can be done. In our own country there is much disrespect, bitterness and violence among us at the moment. There are people entrenched in their 'nests' who do not want to fly. As a result, we are gripped by a malaise and nothing moves.

Perhaps, how hard it is to say it, we have not suffered enough? Sometimes change only seems to come when the alternative is the destruction of what I have. There is simply no other way forward. You have to change or die. It seems that our rulers feel that they have not reached this stage: that they can go on as they are indefinitely. The question that we are asking now is how much more of our country has to be destroyed before change and reconciliation becomes the only way forward. How many more have to suffer violence – both the victims and the perpetrators are affected – before we awaken to what we are doing to our society and our children.

24 August, 2008

102

SIMEON AND THE VISIT

Occasionally someone comes along who catches our imagination because he or she represents the best in us. In the 1930s many saw Gandhi as one such person and in the 1990s, Mandela. The world figure of the moment must be Obama. It is hard to find a critical word said about him. He is on a global honeymoon.

Churchill is said to have remarked that democracy is a poor form of government but it is the best we have. Perhaps what he meant was that in the end it all comes down to one man or woman. If you have someone who represents the best in each of us, you have the best form of government possible.

I had such thoughts as I noticed the season of Advent coming round again like a planet in orbit. What is so wonderful about this time before Christmas? Jewish history in the Old Testament doesn't have a happy ending. All their kings and prophets couldn't prevent them from sinking into being an insignificant province of an empire that reached from Iraq to the Atlantic. And yet there was something magnificent in the last words written about this old dispensation. In the early pages of Luke there were a few people still around to voice the peak of longing of the Jewish people: 'Oh that you would tear the heavens open and come down' (Isaiah 63:!9). And the one, to my mind, who surely represents the best of that old world was Simeon. He was a devout traditional Jew who frequented the temple but was also among the first to recognise there was something new happening.

'Blessed be the Lord, the God of Israel, for he has visited his people,' he found himself saying (Luke 1:68 and 78), echoing that earlier visit when Moses spoke God's message to the elders of Israel, 'I have visited you and seen all that the Egyptians are doing to you' (Exodus 4:16). In that little word 'visit', Simeon proclaims an event that has changed our world forever. We'd all love a visitor – Thabo Mbeki, Kofi Annan – to solve our problems. Often they can't. But at a profound level – I know this sounds a little remote from experience – we have a visitor who has promised to stay 'to the end of time' (Matt 28:20), that is until everything is sorted out.

This 'visit' is still on even if we are not aware of it, preoccupied as we are with inflation, starvation, lack of education and medication and all the other '-ations' that make up our nation. If we read Simeon's words we will see how they sum up the best of our desires. He does not promise a quick fix but it is more like a long haul. What Advent reminds us of each year is that we can reach out beyond what holds us down. We have a permanent visitor with us.

30 November, 2008

103

JOY AND TEARS

Marion is happy. He sings and dances. And the reason? He has just been baptised. Marion is an epileptic and because he was always falling into the fire his hands became burnt and eventually what was left of them had to be amputated. So he cannot do much for himself; but he is happy. He carries his food awkwardly on his head, but he doesn't feel sorry for himself. He just manages somehow and he smiles. He is like someone who has conquered the world. It can do no more harm to him.

Recently some professional people 'came away to a lonely place for a while' (Mark 6:31) and spent a day or two in quiet. Entering into their own hearts and seeing what was there some of them shed tears. These were not the tears of sorrow for themselves but the tears of realisation, of forgiveness and of freedom. It was painful to face the truth but once they did it they, like Marion, felt their joy released. 'Their joy was so great that they could not believe it' (Luke 24:41).

Joy and tears are gifts and they are close to one another. To come to one is often to come to the other. Don Bosco grew up in Italy at the time of the industrial revolution when whole families disintegrated as people crowded into the cities in search of a better life. The children were forgotten in this modern exodus and had to live by their wits. Bosco felt his call was to reach out to them and help. But they rebuffed him and turned away. He tried to befriend the kids time and again but without success. One day, in their presence, he burst into tears; tears of frustration. And those tears opened the door to those children's hearts. The rest is history: Bosco and his friends (who became the Salesians, after Francis de Sales) went on to build technical and academic schools and orphanages for boys all over the world. In Africa there is a huge 'youth city' in Lubumbashi and also in many other parts of the continent.

So when we are reduced to tears, as so many are these days, it can be painful but it can also be a door to a new way of seeing or being seen and such revelations can bring joy.

9 February, 2009

104

A LITTLE BIT

People interviewed in Bulawayo over the Government of National Unity said it gave them 'a little bit of hope'. The MDC are putting a brave face on the continued foot-dragging and even hostility shown to them. When Tendai Biti was asked whether he would forgive and forget there was a long pause before he answered. Then he said he could forgive, but not forget. 'Never again in this country should the government act like a bunch of bandits.'

The big test will be when work starts in earnest next week. Will the various parties show endless passive aggression towards each other or will they rise above themselves and put the issues of the country first? Is there a chance that they will work together for the common good? It is one thing to have huge problems facing you when you enter government such as those Barack Obama has. It is quite another when, on top of the problems, you have your own colleagues in government sabotaging your every move. This happened in South Africa after 1994 when staff prevented new ministers from doing their work.

So our new government of 'fire and ice', of internal contradictions, sets out with people wondering what chance it has of achieving. There is so much to be 'unlearned'. I first read of that word in a lecture by the President of Ireland about the agreement in the North of her country. And she gave an example of her own children, as it were leading the way. Her five-year-old said to her one day, 'Mommy, is it true we are divided between Protestants and Catholics?' 'Yes, Sally, that's right,' said the mother; to which the little girl replied, 'and which are we, I forget?'

Northern Ireland has dropped from the headlines because the two formerly hostile parties that form the government there are working together. Good news isn't news. Is it possible that we are moving in some such similar direction? Is it possible that one of our ministers' small children will soon ask his father, 'which are we, I forget?' Today that moment seems some way off. But maybe, maybe, we can still afford to hope.

13 February, 2009

105

SOMETHING NEW

When news came in the dark days of Second World War that the allies had secured a victory in North Africa, Churchill is reported to have damped down enthusiasm by saying, 'this is not the beginning of the end but it is perhaps the end of the beginning.' There is definitely a different mood in this country today from what there was even two weeks ago and for that we can be thankful. But no one is presuming that this is the beginning of the end of our troubles.

There is, however, an interesting process underway. Normally in any organisation there are structures and lines of command; everyone knows who they are answerable to. In our situation – and it must be unique – these lines are blurred and those in government may be competing with one another. It is possible that alliances and party loyalties may weaken in the face of the need to get things done. Certainly, as an observer, it seems the Prime Minister does not expect to have his own way automatically and realises that he will have to push every inch of the way. Maybe, after years of waiting, that is just the sort of struggle that will energise him.

The situation is so unclear that it is possible that at the end of the day everyone could turn out to be a winner. If those in authority really focus on what has to be done – and heed the words of the prophet – they, and we, could be in for a big surprise!

No need to recall the past,

> *no need to think about what was done before.*
> *See, I am doing a new deed,*
> *even now it comes to light; can you not see it?*
> (Isaiah 43: 18-1.)

We are entering into a new time where anything can happen. If we can just take hold of it, not with any selfish intention, but with courage to see this matter succeed; then we will see something marvellous emerge. I heard recently of some of the perpetrators of violence last year coming forward, wanting to reach out for reconciliation with their victims. I would say that is not unusual. I am sure there are lots of people just waiting for an opportunity to reach across the divides that we have built to work together. There must hardly be a person, from the Zambezi to the Limpopo, who wants this country to fail however differently they interpret success. With so much good will, is it not possible to establish a new beginning?

22 February, 2009

106

LAYING HOLD OF HOPE

If the events of the past two weeks have taught us anything it is about the fragility of our lives – and the unpredictability of the future. Anything can happen any time. No one could think that, in addition to all the pressures on him, the Prime Minister would lose his wife so abruptly and his children, their mother.[4] And few could imagine that such an event would throw a spark into our political traffic jam. The President visited the Prime Minister after the accident and then went to the funeral church service. He said things there that he might never have said otherwise and one member of the family marvelled. A few words on the part of a leading figure do not necessarily change everything but they can be the indication of a desire to rise above the gridlock we daily endure.

When I expressed such comments to a colleague I received a vehement rebuff. The President is always saying things that suit the occasion, he said, and he never really means them. He reminded me of his swords into ploughshares speech in 1980 that was followed a little later by Gukurahundi.

He may be right. This colleague is a seasoned follower of events. But I still believe we have to hold on to wisps of hope however fleeting they may be. There is no one so bad that there is not some good in them; just as there is no one so good that he or

---

4   Susan Tsvangirai was killed in a collision on the Harare-Masvingo Road on 6 March, 2009.

she does not have a shadow side. People can change and shocking events can often be a catalyst that opens a door. Martin Luther King's death may have done more to deepen the commitment of American blacks to struggle for their rights than all his eloquent words while he was alive. When a person dies suddenly and tragically in the midst of her ordinary duties you are forced to look at her life. Many tributes have been paid to Susan Tsvangirai but what stands out is her daily engagement in the life and struggles of her husband. The death of such a person sends ripples around civil society and touches everyone, even the highest in the land. And if someone shows even a small desire to change, even at a late stage, is it not right to welcome that?

The past is unalterable but full of lessons. The present is unpredictable. But the future is wide open for us to make. We can stroll casually into it and 'see what happens' or we can lay hold of it and make things happen. Any word, any gesture, any work that points to a future which takes us out of our present jam is welcome and invites us to build on it.

13 March, 2009

107

REBUILDING

Kalemie is the name of a small town in the Democratic Republic of Congo on the western shore of Lake Tanganyika. Close by was a centre the Arabs used as a base for gathering slaves and moving them on to Zanzibar, the island off the coast of Tanzania. Later, during the colonial period, Kalemie became a bustling commercial centre at the head of the railway that ran west to the Congo river. Goods could then travel across the lake to the east coast of the continent. Today Kalemie hardly exists. The railway track is long since overgrown. There are no roads passable for vehicles out of the town and clean water and regular electricity are a memory. Corruption and war in the eastern Congo have devastated the economic and social infrastructure and so also the lives of the people.

Kalemie's story in one way or another can be repeated up and down the continent, beginning perhaps with the overgrown roads and aqueducts of Roman North Africa. Much of our country is 'overgrown' and also in decay. But what is amazing – and we are just coming to this period – is how people can find the strength and fortitude to rebuild.

Pope Benedict has just issued a stirring appeal to the millions who gathered to celebrate the Eucharist with him in Luanda. Addressing the young people in particular he called them to rebuild their country after the decades of independence and then the civil war.[5] There are people in Angola who have never known anything but war until recently.[6]

Despite the economic downturn in the world economy there is a real desire to build something new on the ashes of the present. People have hope.

> *By the rivers of Babylon*
> *we sat down and wept*

These words of Psalm 137 are not the end of the story. Close on their heels come the words of Cyrus, king of Persia (2 Chronicles 36:23):

'The Lord, the God of Heaven, has ordered me to build him a temple in Jerusalem. Whoever there is among you of all his people, may his God be with him! Let him go up.'

The joy of rebuilding the temple in the Old Testament times is a symbol of the joy we have in rebuilding our world.

21 March, 2009

---

5   The Democratic Republic of Congo is slowly recovering from a conflict known as Africa's first world war, which led to the loss of some five million lives between 1994 and 2003, but many eastern areas are still plagued by violence as various rebel groups continue to operate there. (Wikipedia)
6   The Angolan Civil War was a major civil conflict in Angola, beginning in 1975 and continuing, with some interludes, until 2002. The war began immediately after Angola became independent from Portugal in November 1975. (Wikipedia)

108

COVERED IN GLORY

'Glory,' like love, truth or freedom, is a much-used word. But what is it? It was or is a moment of glory when Nelson Mandela emerged from prison after 28 years, or when Barack Obama won the election in the United States or when Didier Drobga displays his skill on the football field. But what is glory? Towards the end of John's gospel (18:24), Jesus says to his Father:

> I want those you have given me
> to be with me where I am,
> so that they may always see the glory
> You have given me
> because you loved me
> before the foundation of the world.

In the Old Testament the glory of God was so overwhelming that Moses had to cover his face (Exodus 3:6). But in the New Testament the glory seems more manageable. John speaks a lot about it. At the wedding feast of Cana 'he let his glory be seen' (2:11) and there is no report of people covering their faces. But that is the essence of God becoming one of us: he becomes accessible – and so does his glory. In 12:23 we have the solemn declaration, 'now the hour has come for the Son of Man to be glorified' and what he means is to go through the most painful physical and mental suffering – the worst that human life can throw at any man or woman – and to overcome it.

It was precisely in his torment and death that he achieved glory.

We have come a long way from the dazzling manifestations of Exodus. We see Jesus 'despised and rejected ... a man of sorrows ... a man to make people screen their faces' (Isaiah 53), not because of his brightness but because of his disfigurement and humiliation.

Glory is when a person does not run away from conflict and engagement but enters into it and comes out on top. It can be my choice when I become involved in some work that brings change to people's lives. Or it can be something I don't choose but I accept with courage and patience, knowing I can't do anything about it. Bryce Courtenay is an Australian who wrote a book[7] about his son Damon who suffered from leukaemia and went through endless operations with moments of hope and moments of near despair. In the end, Damon died but the doctor said:

> *'You know, Bryce, Damon wasn't just an ordinary young man; he had more heart, more guts, more character and more courage than any patient I've ever treated. He never complained; he always had great dignity and he taught me a great deal. As far as I am concerned, he died absolutely covered in glory.'*

'Covered in glory!' That may be how we see Mandela or Obama or any other great figure of our time. But is it how we see the man dying of AIDS who has struggled to 'live positively' or the woman who rises early and struggles all day that her children can have food, clothing and education? We are all called to glory. Most of us are not called to Obama-like glory nor the Damon sort. But to enter into life with all its challenges without running away and seeking our comfort: that is open to all of us.

28 May, 2009

---

7   *April Fool's Day* by Bryce Courtenay. Penguin Books, Australia, 1998.

4

THE INSPIRATION OF PEOPLE

109

JOHN BRADBURNE OF MUTEMWA

John Bradburne was killed beside the Mutoko Nyamapanda road on 5 September, 1979. He was buried on the 10th, the day the Lancaster House Conference, which ended the war, opened in London. The events could hardly be further apart in place or in purpose but at the time their coincidence was deeply significant.

This explains the enormous appeal of John in recent years. Despite fuel shortages people make their way to Mutemwa each September in their thousands. And throughout the year smaller groups gather there. They sense it is a holy place where they can come together to pray for the country and gather strength to go on. They spend the whole night on Chigona Mountain listening, singing, praying and celebrating the Eucharist.

We know that besides civic and political activity there is a need to call on God if we are to build a just society. It is not enough to call on God alone. It has to go together with work if the true peace we thought Lancaster would bring is to finally arrive.

No one sensed this better than John. He was a searcher all his life. It would be easy to say he was a searcher for God but that neatly parcels him and removes him from the day-to-day tumble of life. Born in the beautiful hill county of Cumbria in England in 1921, he travelled in war and in peace to many countries and places searching for what he wanted. In the end he wrote:

God's love within you is your native land.
So search none other, never more depart.
For you are homeless save God keeps your heart.

He eventually found the place where he could be content: among the people of Mutemwa who suffered – and continue to suffer – from leprosy. There he tended their needs for food and medicine and he led them each day in prayer and song in the little chapel for ten years until the night of his abduction, which led to his killing.

Over the years since his death John has become known in many parts of the world. Recognising his closeness to God people seek his help and there are many accounts of help received.[1] John was a gift to Zimbabwe in that he shone out as a person of unwavering integrity. At the same time he made each one - friend and 'enemy' alike - feel good about themselves. 'Never fail / to think of knaves as kings Christ dreams to crown.' And finally there was always humour – that great sign of inner freedom.

19 October, 2005

1   www.johnbradburne.com

110

MARLA RUZICKA

We quickly recognise the courage of individuals and their achievements. A news account that lacks personal stories soon fades from memory. In Zimbabwe, we thirst for a lead from individuals who can make a difference. When we find one we are inspired: we celebrate and broadcast their exploits. Amongst us are countless heroes. There is a woman in the Shamva area who takes care of AIDS patients at home, speaking frankly, she said:

> *There are three very sick people just in this village. The situation forces me to go three or four times a day to help them stay clean. We have no painkiller or any sort of drugs. I do not have any protective clothing. I am now very worried about my health and concerned for my children. Sometimes I feel useless. The families' problems are too much: sick parents, hungry children in tattered clothes, no schooling and no work.*

But this person carries on day after day without pay, tending to the sick in her midst, people who are not her relatives.

The *Guardian Weekly* recently published a story about 'Bubbles of Kabul':[2] Marla Ruzicka was a young American girl in her twenties and she earned her nickname by her fearless effervescent probing about civilian casualties in the American assaults on Afghanistan and Iraq. She became convinced that the US government was simply ignoring the 'collateral damage'

2   20 April, 2005

it was doing and she travelled to areas where others feared to go in search of accurate figures of civilians caught up in conflict. 'The US embassy (in Kabul) loathed Marla, not least for the day she assembled dozens of mostly Pashtun tribesmen, some bandaged and limping in front of its walls to demand compensation.'[3]

Marla moved to Iraq at the time of the US and British attack and mobilised volunteers to visit hospitals to find out the real number of casualties. 'A number is important,' she wrote, 'not only to quantify the cost of war but to me each number is also a story of someone whose hopes, dreams and potential will never be realised, and who left behind a family.'[4]

Marla and her Iraqi colleague, Faiz Al Salaam, were killed in one of those seemingly endless attacks we hear of each day in Iraq on 16 April, 2005. She was 29 years old. Her last words to the medic who treated her were 'I'm alive'.

The first unnamed Zimbabwean woman makes no headlines. The second, Marla, burst onto the world's screens in the days after her death. Both gave everything they had that others might live.

12 May, 2005

---

3   Ibid.
4   Ibid.

111

A CARING NURSE

A friend of mine was so touched by the care of a nurse recently that he composed a letter and circulated it to share his New Year joy. Good news is not something we have come to expect. It can be unsettling, as we are so inured to bad news in Zimbabwe.

My friend had had a serious accident towards the end of 2005 and he and his fellow travellers were initially cared for in a government hospital in Mutoko. They received the best care possible, but more than that, the nurse who cared for them phoned several of them after they had left hospital to find out how they were getting on.

It is common knowledge that our hospitals are struggling. The government itself described Parirenyatwa last year as being 'in intensive care'. Supplies are hard to come by and nurses are not paid a living wage. The morale among nurses suffers as a result. Just this week a baby died in a hospital in Harare because at a critical moment after birth there was no one in attendance on the mother.

Yet this particular nurse rose above all the limitations of her job and situation to reach out to someone who was hurt and badly shaken by his experience. She decided a long time ago not to give in to the general discouragement in the profession but to make her own way and set her own ideals. In her family life she felt herself blessed by God and in return decided, in my friend's words, 'to do her job to the very best of her abilities'. What a simple everyday expression and yet what a powerful one! She cared for the bodies of the wounded people but much more she touched their hearts. The poet Yeats has a line about someone who

> *Wild with divinity*
> *Had so lit up the whole...*

There is no more powerful incentive than the witness of action, which goes against – or rises above – the normal. It releases something within us. We catch fire. We can call this quality 'leadership.'

11 January, 2006

112

ELIZABETH MUSODZI

The constant phrase, *toitei*? (what can we do?) with its response *hapana* (nothing) is becoming our habitual attitude. Hopes that once resided in civic society or political opposition have melted. Hopelessness has taken over. There is a feeling our leaders no longer respect us. They are now laughing at us. They have us where they want us: helpless and submissive. The best we can do is simply to survive and wait for better days.

If there is some truth in this diagnosis we need some symbols of hope to lift our spirits. We know there are women today – Netsai Mushonga[5] for example – who do give us hope. But sometimes their names and deeds get buried in the mass of news and documentation which is our daily fare and which lulls us into directionless confusion.

So it is salutary to remember when other figures stood up against the prevailing climate. Japanese historian Tsuneo Yoshikuni has made a study of Mai Musodzi, a resident of Harare in the 1920s, '30s and '40s. Over half the entire population (3,837) of the 'location' turned out to her funeral in 1952. The *African Weekly* of 6 August that year called her '*amai* to every African in the township.'

Musodzi was born c. 1885 in the Gomba Valley south of the present Mazowe Dam and her family was part of Chief Hwata's people who were active in the first chimurenga. She lost her

---

5 A women's rights, gender and peacebuilding activist.

parents in the fighting and sought refuge with Chief Chinamhora who placed her under the care of the Dominican Sisters at the newly opened Chishawasha Mission. There she learnt many practical skills and met her future husband, Frank Kashimbo Ayema, a member of the BSAP and who came from Barotseland.

The 1920s were difficult times for blacks as the colonial government squeezed out competitive entrepreneurs. In 1924, Musodzi was already producing, 'five bags of mealies, five bags of monkey nuts, five bags of rice, 50 pumpkins and 35 bags of rapoko'.[6] She was poised to compete with commercial farmers. And what is more, her example was being followed by other women who were despairing of their marriages and looking for divorces as their husbands did not share their wages with their families. An elderly Hararian told Yoshikuni, 'most marriages survived because of this woman'.[7] She helped them to be self-reliant.

Mai Musodzi went on to start the African Women's Clubs and she introduced 'true nursing' through the Red Cross. A few lines here cannot do due justice to this woman but it is clear that she was an inspiration to the Harare community for over three decades. Even the Governor General recognised it, as he invited Ma Musodzi to meet the Queen at a dinner in 1947.

Mai Musodzi is not included when the heroes of Zimbabwe are recalled, nor is she buried in their Acre. But she gave an example to her generation because she got up and did things that lit a fire in others. When the fire blazes there is no sign of the original match but there was one.

14 March, 2006

---

6 *Elizabeth Musodzi and the Birth of African Feminism in Early Colonial Zimbabwe* by Tsuneo Yoshikuni. Weaver Press & Silveira House, Harare, 2008 p.12.
7 Ibid.

113

BENEDICT XVI

Pope Benedict has chosen to write his first universal letter on love. It has been greeted very positively, even among those who have nothing to do with the Catholic Church. There, on the pages of the world's papers, which deal so much with violence, hatred, fraud and revenge, is an article about a world leader who writes about love.

No one can object because everyone knows that the most fundamental thing about our existence is our desire to love and be loved. Still, the pope is quite daring, at least in traditional Catholic eyes, in speaking about *eros* as the first wellspring of love. This Greek word, source of the word erotic, only appears twice in the scriptures, he tells us, and both times in the Old Testament. But Benedict is determined to trace love from its origins to its goal. *Eros*, he says, represents an indeterminate 'searching' love, whilst *agape* – another Greek word – is the typical expression of the biblical notion of love 'which involves a real discovery of the other. So love, that most powerful force that 'makes the world go round,' has to move from *eros* to *agape*, from self-centredness to concern for another person or for other people. It is purified through life's difficulties and often considerable suffering.

Pope Benedict moves on to the implications of love for our human society. Love is meaningless unless it is expressed in action for justice. The traditional Marxist analysis viewed charity as a pernicious way of delaying revolutionary change. It salved the conscience of the rich to give something from their wealth to the poor. In so doing, the rich blunted the anger of the poor and oppressed. There is some truth in this. But what kind of love would it be, if we let the hungry starve so that, in theory, the revolution takes place sooner? Surely, we have both to respond to suffering now, *and* work for justice now. Truly, says Benedict, creating a just society is the work of politics and the Church cannot do it. But the Church has to proclaim the demand for justice. He quotes Augustine of Hippo[8] who wrote, *remota itaque iustitia quid sunt regna nisi magna latrocinia*, a government that does not function according to justice is just a bunch of thieves. Benedict continues: The Church cannot and must not take upon herself the political battle to bring about the most just society possible. She cannot and must not replace the State. Yet at the same time she cannot and must not remain on the sidelines in the fight for justice. She has to play her part through rational argument and she has to awaken the spiritual energy without which justice, which always demands sacrifice, cannot prevail and prosper. A just society must be the achievement of politics, not of the Church. Yet the promotion of justice through efforts to bring about openness of mind and will to the demands of the common good is something that concerns the Church deeply.

There was a recent article in *The Herald* trying to isolate Archbishop Pius Ncube from his fellow bishops. What the writer fails to understand is that the archbishop is expressing the mind of the Church and his whole life is an act of selfless love.

28 February 2006

---

8   Augustine of Hippo (354–430), also known as Saint Augustine, was an early Christian theologian and philosopher whose writings influenced the development of Western Christianity and Western philosophy. He was the bishop of Hippo Regius (modern-day Annaba, Algeria). He is viewed as one of the most important Church Fathers in Western Christianity. Among his most important works are *The City of God* and *Confessions*.

114

SALLY MUGABE

Recently I visited a woman who talked happily about general issues for a time: how long she had lived with her family, how far away the well was and so on. Then her husband came and we settled into the business of my visit, which was connected with their marriage. Suddenly the woman was in tears, deep inconsolable tears. I looked at the husband and he was laughing. I could excuse him and say he was embarrassed and did not know what to say or do and took refuge in laughter. But sadly the thought came to me, and would not go away; he is laughing at her.

I felt overwhelmed with the burden this woman carried and indeed so many women in Africa carry. And, no doubt, it is true elsewhere. Despite modernity and the breakdown of ancient ways, women are still in thrall to heartless men. When they marry they cross a line and their lives depend upon the sort of person their husband is. If the love he declares means respect, mutual forgiveness, fidelity and sharing decisions, there is every hope he and his wife will live happily together. But if he opts for dominance, lording it over her, going his own way, there is still – in 2006 – little she can do unless she is a tough lady who tolerates no nonsense and can fight her corner.

If he is the dominating type his wife may feel she has no alternative but to settle for a life of patient endurance. To this will be added deep anxiety about her children should her husband contract HIV. Fr Michael Kelly of Lusaka, who has become an acknowledged international expert in alerting us to the implications of HIV and AIDS, says AIDS is basically a man's disease the consequences of which are borne by women.

There is a stirring in the mix we call society and women are speaking up all over the world, so much so that in the rich world men are said to be losing confidence in themselves and their identity. Whatever anxious truth there may be in this, the fact remains that our women continue to bear the burdens of some of the more oppressive aspects of tradition. They also, of course, 'bear' all of us. In one of his more chauvinist moments, when he is basically saying the fall in the Garden of Eden was all Eve's fault, St Paul says, 'nevertheless (a woman) will be saved by childbearing' (I Tim 2:15). Paul's meaning seems to be that the mediation and nourishment of life confers an unspeakable dignity on women.

Years ago I attended meetings where Sally Mugabe, in her work with women, used to join in the fashion of slogans. *'Pamberi nemadzimai!'* she would shout, *'madzimai,* we are oppressed by our husbands!' One presumes she was speaking from general, not personal, experience. But her message remains.

2 April 2006

The Inspiration of People

115

LUISA GUIDOTTI

'There are lies, damned lies and then there are statistics,' Churchill is said to have snorted when some bad news was brought to him. We have our fill of all three but they don't change hearts. Take statistics. We now know that we have the lowest life expectancy (37 years for men and 34 years for women), the highest rate of inflation (782%, followed by Iraq at 40%) and the fastest declining economy in the world. We know that malnutrition is widespread and that people are dying of hunger although sometimes they die of AIDS before they actually starve to death.

All these facts are well documented. Indeed some of them appear in the government-controlled press. Yet the same government is in denial consistently refusing to acknowledge the extent of the suffering or to welcome help from all sides to alleviate it. In fact they are doing the opposite as numerous reports show:

'Children in ragged clothes clamour for food while women sit around with dulled expressions, chewing seeds. Many have been affected mentally, according to Pastor Edwin. 'Whenever I try to sleep, I see my wardrobe being smashed and my house going up in flames,' said one woman. Every few days police come and chase them out again, but they have nowhere else to go. 'We're losing an average of two people a week here to starvation,' said the pastor, showing some abandoned shelters where the inhabitants have died. 'Several times I've been called to places urgently, only to find they have already died of starvation. I see the signs everywhere - the hands and feet grey like bark.' The government doesn't care about these people.'[9]

We are celebrating Easter. Celebrating? Luisa Guidotti was the doctor in All Souls Mutoko Mission hospital during the war. She used to treat everyone including guerillas who came by night. And then the soldiers would interrogate her by day. She lived a terrible tension. A few days before government soldiers killed her, she came to our house and walked round and round a small table almost overcome by the tension, the Gethsemane, she was living. Earlier she had come for a weekend of reflection and with her beaming Italian smile and broken English said, 'do not talk to me of the Passion. I have it everyday. Speak to me of the Resurrection!'[10]

How can we speak of the Resurrection in the midst of our suffering? After Gethsemane, the classic scriptural narrative of exile, alienation and suffering is Babylon. By its waters 'we sat and wept. ... How could we sing one of Yahweh's songs in an alien land?' (Psalm 137) How can you celebrate Easter in the midst of this dreadful affliction of the people of Zimbabwe? There is no easy answer, except to say that it is through struggling while trying to remain honest and upright that we come to new life. Everywhere in this country today there are people doing just that. They are planting the seeds of a new society. Most to be pitied are those who live a daily lie, concocting strategies of survival, which have no foundation in the truth of what most people live.

9 April, 2006

---

9   *Sunday Times* (UK), 2 April, 2006.

10   Luisa Guidotti Mistrali (1932-79) an Italian doctor and missionary who put people not politics first. On 6 July 1979 while she was accompanying a sick pregnant woman to Nyadiri hospital, the car was hit by gunfire and she died. The assailants are unknown.

116

RAYMOND KAPITO

In the early hours of Monday, 10 April, Raymond Kapito, a Jesuit priest, finally succumbed to ill health. He died 'with his boots on,' as Fr Fidelis Mukonori said in his sermon, having just agreed to yet another posting, at the age of 78, to Mazowe where he was involved in the spiritual formation of future priests. Fr Kapito was mourned – celebrated might be a better word – by so many people during an all night *pungwe* and the funeral the next day that it is worth writing a word about him for a wider readership.

'He was a typical African,' Fr Fidelis – told us, referring to his being rooted in his strong traditional rural background in Mutoko and his confident ability to build other values he learnt in life from many sources onto this foundation.

A dominant influence grafted onto these roots was the rigorous formation of the Catholic seminary in the 1940s. Raymond's formal education did not consist of degrees and doctorates but he grew into a rock-like assurance of who he was as an African Christian with a mission. The stories over these days of celebration all point to a man of solid principles, which he lived and transmitted to others tirelessly. 'He never judged anyone,' we were told and this means that individuals in our country – even the highest in the land – were not condemned as people. But he was straightforward and even ruthless about ways of behaving that were eating into the core of society. His grandmother once confronted a lion and chased it from their homestead. Raymond too would confront other lions in his long life and send them running.

Countless people, but especially priests in training, came under his relentless proclamation of the values of life: honesty, integrity, openness and forgiveness. He would prance about the place entertaining people – a laugh a minute – but the message was transmitted.

'A typical African!' Is that a fact or a wish? To be 'typical' means there must be many of that type. Regrettably, Fr Kapito was somewhat unique. Men or women like him are not peopling this land today. So the phrase means he represented the best in a solid and rich tradition. May his influence live on after him and produce more like him in the new society struggling to be born!

12 April, 2006

MOSES

We have just buried Moses. Actually it was the second time he was buried. The first time was in 1992 in a forest near Chinhoyi. His unknown mother must have panicked on the day of his birth and half buried him in a remote spot. A passer-by heard his cries and took him to Chinhoyi hospital where the nurses cared for him for five years. He bled a lot at his birth as his umbilical cord was not treated and he suffered severe brain and bodily damage. The nurses could not find a place that would care for him and just kept him in the ward.

In 1997 a house opened its doors in Harare with the express aim of welcoming mentally disabled people and offering them as near a normal home as possible. The people who run l'Arche, as it is called – the Ark of Noah, a place of refuge and hope – want to create a 'family' for people who have been abandoned for one reason or another or whose own family just cannot cope. The aim is not just to provide the basics of life – food, shelter, medical care, etc. – but to create a place where the handicapped can develop their own unique gifts. So everyone at l'Arche shares in the shopping, gardening, candle-making, cooking, washing and cleaning, etc. Gradually the handicapped people discover friendship and security and they begin to blossom. They begin to share their gifts and this can have a profound effect on those who come to live with them. In the all night *pungwe* for Moses, speaker after speaker told of the effect of this little fourteen-year-old boy on their lives. He could not speak or do anything for himself but he related to people in a powerful way. People spoke of how they came to l'Arche a bit sad that all they could find was a job with these handicapped people. Some felt angry and frustrated and the pay was little. But gradually over time if they learnt to stop and take time in relating to Moses something amazing would happen. It was obvious he had no interest in those who passed by and said, 'Hi Mosi! *Uri bho?*' and moved on. They just got a vacant stare. But if someone stopped, and tried to 'learn his language,' gradually their lives were touched. Moses taught us a lot about relating to people and in doing so he taught us about relating to Jesus. This 'useless' little guy did a great deal in his 14 years!

L'Arche was founded in France in 1964 by Jean Vanier, a French Canadian who had been in the navy and had also taught philosophy in Toronto. He was 35 and despite what he had already achieved in life he knew he was called to more. Now 77, he often speaks of how he found what he searched for with two disabled people, Raphael and Philippe, in the village of Trosly, 100 km north of Paris. He welcomed them into a little house he had bought. Over time others joined him and new communities were formed. Today, 42 years later, there are some 120 communities of l'Arche worldwide.[11] Jean travels a good deal and has been to Zimbabwe four times in the past 25 years. In his talks he has often mentioned Moses and at the World Youth Day in Canada in 2002, before thousands of young people, he gave the full story. Yesterday, although he never knew it, we buried an international star.

10 August, 2006

---

11   www.larche.org

118

ARCHBISHOP PIUS NCUBE

The Herald, 17 July, and for days afterwards, gives extensive coverage to an alleged affair between Archbishop Pius Ncube and Mrs Rosemary Sibanda. The report brings a sense of shock and sadness to Zimbabweans and particularly to Catholics. For any public figure to be seen to break the trust of the people who look up to him or her is bad enough. But for a religious leader, whose very role is to foster the intimate bond between God and his people, it is doubly painful. The Catholic Church has developed a practice of celibacy for her clergy and members of religious communities over the centuries. It is a practice she has stuck to despite its rejection by the Reformed Churches and those that came after them. The practice is directly related to the service of God and his people.

Anyone who tries to live this life will tell you it is a struggle. Just because you embrace a life of celibacy does not mean that you become any different from other people of flesh and blood. You still feel the yearnings of being human. Yet is God calls you to this way of life you believe that he does it for a purpose and will give what it takes to live it.

And if, on top of such a struggle, a person walks a lonely road of speaking out against injustice, when most people keep quiet, the burden and the struggle can become too much to bear. The article on the middle page of *The Herald* carries a vehement attack on the archbishop, not because of his alleged affair of which the writer seems unaware, but because of his struggle for justice. Archbishop Ncube has taken a big risk to speak out the way he has and his message has been heard. We know that because, far from being ignored, he has often been roundly condemned in the media on his stand.

If the allegation is true, it will do great damage to him and to the church and indeed to the country. Yet the media seems to relish his humiliation. Shakespeare says 'you rub the sore// When you should bring the plaster'.[12] If these sad events are true, it is a time for compassion, prayer and rebuilding. It is not a time for gloating and 'I told you so'.

If a great man stumbles he does not cease to be a great man. Perhaps he has paid a heavy price for the very things that made him so admired. Perhaps the personal cost was just too much. Whatever is the truth about this matter, and many believe that photos can be doctored and created on the computer, one thing is for certain: Archbishop Pius Ncube is now entering a period of much suffering. He deserves all the support and understanding we can give him. When Paul was boasting about all that he had endured in his mission he went on to say that 'to stop me getting too proud I was given a thorn in the flesh... I pleaded with the Lord... and he said, "my grace is enough for you" my power is at its best in weakness' (2 Cor. 12:7). Experiencing weakness can be a step towards deep conversion – both for individuals and for the church and indeed for the country.

19 July, 2007

---

12   *The Tempest*, Act 2 Scene 1.

119

LUCKY DUBE AND DORIS LESSING

Paul faced much opposition when he reached Europe. In Philippi, Thessalonika and Athens he was either insulted, flogged, derided or imprisoned. One night in Corinth he was encouraged by the Lord, 'do not be afraid to speak out ... I am with you. I have so many people on my side in this city' (Acts 18:10). The people 'on side' in the city were not priests or ministers of religion. They were ordinary people who could recognise truth when they saw it.

This past week two people, reared on the soil of Southern Africa have hit the world headlines. Lucky Dube, the reggae star, was shot in an attempted car highjack in Johannesburg. His death has saddened many people and it has also brought his life and work into perspective. While he entertained he also challenged us to recognise hard truths. It is one thing to reach agreements and shake hands. It is quite another to deeply respect other people – especially those who are different. One of Lucky Dube's messages was 'without respect there is no progress'.

When we think back to Zimbabwe in 1980 we remember how black and white, Shona and Ndebele shook hands and agreed to work together. 'Yesterday you were my enemy, today ...' and all that. But was there deep respect? People worked together in the same office or factory but come the end of the day they each returned to their own ghetto. Segregation, with its undertone of mistrust, reasserted itself soon after the ink was dry on the declaration of independence.

Doris Lessing has just been awarded the Nobel prize for literature – an honour recognised as the highest humankind have yet devised. She was born in 1920 and grew up in a Southern Rhodesia which she considered the most 'culturally boring' place imaginable. 'The main topic of conversation among whites was the latest misdeeds of their black servants.' Prompted by an article in a newspaper which reported the arrest of a 'houseboy' on a farm she wrote *The Grass is Singing*, a novel about a white woman in an impossible marriage who comes under the influence of her black servant, Moses. There are sexual undertones – enough to alarm the white minority who promptly had the book withdrawn from the shops – but they are not the main point. The housewife is caught in a tension; she should assert her 'superiority' over this servant but at the same time she discovered her need for him. He gave her some kind of solidity in her otherwise pointless life. Lessing punctured the myths of white supremacy in a way that enraged the then rulers of South Africa and Southern Rhodesia.

'I have so many people on my side.' Some are derided, exiled, tortured or shot. But there are many who speak up for truth. Lucky Dube and Doris Lessing are in the headlines but wherever someone recognises truth and has the courage to speak it he or she is 'on my side' and in good company.

22 October 2007

120

MICHAEL IVENS: SUFFERING CAN TRANSFORM US

Michael Ivens died in Wales a few years ago. About ten years previously a brain tumour was discovered and it was pressing on the optic nerve. As time went by a risky operation was proposed: it might save his sight but in so doing might cause a stroke and impair his speech. In his own words he had to choose between 'keeping my sight and losing my wits and losing my sight and keeping my wits.' It was a terrible choice the like of which few of us have to make. He chose the latter and duly went blind. He mentioned later 'I am told ninety per cent of blind people can make out something of light and shadow. I'm part of the ten per cent.' He lived his last years in total darkness but with courage, peace and a sense of humour that inspired all around him. He was 'made perfect by suffering' (Hebrews 2:10).

There is just one week in the year that we call 'holy' and this is it. It climaxes in the recall of the events of Jesus' last day when he was betrayed by one of his friends, condemned by his own people and executed by foreigners. We know that he freely gave himself up 'for us.' We may struggle to understand why he had to die. Couldn't he have 'saved' us some other way? What is the link between the cross and our healing? Our scriptures have provided starting points for reflection. One is Isaiah 53:5 'the punishment reconciling us fell on him.' This suggests that he paid the price for our sins. We sinned. He was punished. But where is the link between him and us?

More appealing are the words of Paul in Philippians 2:7. 'he emptied himself ... becoming as we are.' This points to the sharing of experience by Jesus and by us. In his life and in his death he took on everything that it was to be human. His preferred title about himself was 'son of man'. He wanted to be one with us. He entered into our life, experiencing what it is to be human, and because he was who he was in the process he transformed it. Ultimately he transformed death in his rising.

During these days we are invited to set aside time to consider the events and, to use the words of Ignatius Loyola, to 'ponder whatever comes to mind.' It is not necessary, nor indeed possible, to understand fully what the events mean. But we may grasp that to go through suffering as Jesus did may purify and, yes, perfect us. We don't like suffering. No one does. 'Let this cup pass.' But it can transform us. Michael knew that.

March 2008

121

ELIMANE FALL: UNTOUCHED BY POWER

'A catastrophe for the continent!' This phrase was used, not for a new cyclone, or a further outbreak of Ebola, or the moving of the World Cup to Australia. No, it referred to the death by cancer at 53 of the Senegalese journalist, Elimane Fall. The magazine, *Jeune Afrique*, in its 4 May issue, dedicated eleven pages to the tributes about him by statesmen, writers and fellow journalists. Reading through them it is easy to see why they mourn.

Most of us, in English-speaking Africa, have never heard of him. That a famous man can live his life in the French west without even being known in the English south and east is a comment on how divided we remain by history and language. Yet it is worth pondering what people saw in Elimane and why there was so much sorrow at his early departure.

He was completely 'untouched by the seduction of power in Africa.' He did countless interviews with the great and famous – there is a photo of him with an animated Thomas Sankara[13] –

---

13 Thomas Sankara (1949¬–87), was a Burkinabé military captain, Marxist revolutionary, pan-Africanist theorist, and President of Burkina Faso from 1983 to 1987. He is commonly referred to as 'Africa's Che Guevara' because as president he pushed through a social reform programme to benefit ordinary people such as a programme to vaccinate 2.5 million children against meningitis, yellow fever, and measles; outlawing forced marriage, promoting women's rights, etc. He also prohibited bonded labour, and the payment of tributes to chiefs; he insisted his ministers drove small cars and travelled economy class, etc. Needless to say, he was assassinated.

but he was now overawed by the mighty. He kept his eyes on the essential issue and probed and searched for the words that would convey it to his readers. For Elimane Fall public service was always about improving the conditions of life of the people. He looked for nothing for himself except the job well done. In the words of a Malian writer, 'he raised humility to the rank of a doctrine never barricading himself behind impregnable certitudes of his own.'

Journalism was his life and he brought to it intellectual honesty and moral integrity. He was rigorous and personal in his enquiries, but always with a sense of humour. When he met someone from Mali, he would ask for news of the 'people of Bankonin', a reference to the most populous township of the capital, Bamako. It was like someone, eager to find out about conditions in Zimbabwe, asking, 'how are the people of Mbare?'

Another of his colleagues wrote, 'the coups d'état, the corruption, the mediocrity of some African leaders – all these things hurt him deeply. Was it Afro-pessimism? Whatever it was, he did not believe a rebirth would happen quickly.' At the time of the civil war in the Ivory Coast, he was desolated and complained, 'this happens forty years after we became independent. We have learnt nothing.'

We can only glimpse the man from these tributes. But clearly he was someone who was admired and loved. 'He was a good person,' was a verdict that came through and through. He excited people who knew him because of his integrity and courage. Such journalists are the new prophets of our age. Saul trembled before Samuel. Many an African leader did something of the same before Elimane.

15 May, 2008

122

FORWARD TO IMAGINATION!

The accident at Beatrice has shocked us; one because of the bitter blow to the Prime Minister and his family at a time when he is already under so much strain, and two because every accident in Zimbabwe where prominent people are involved is immediately suspected of not being an accident. Reports at present indicate that it really was one, but the mere fact that every car accident is immediately suspect is an indication, once again, of the long road we have still to travel.

I had planned, this week, to write about another death, not of Susan Tsvangirai, but of a person only a handful of people in Zimbabwe know. Yet he should not pass from this world without a word. After all he was the principal builder of Heroes' Acre. Some people devote their lives to music, others to politics. Liam Cotter devoted his to stone. He was passionate about its different textures, uses and qualities. He did the stone work in cathedrals in his time and in his retirement he came out from Ireland to devote years to the painstaking work on building the Acre. When you go there some time to remember the dead, pause for a moment to look at the Chishawasha granite as it gracefully ascends the small hill and becomes a spire reaching to heaven.

Liam Cotter died on the 10 January but the news only filtered through to us last week. A master in his chosen profession he also had an eye for a multitude of other concerns. Just one example will have to serve. There was a well attended night school in

Harare in the 1980s in a difficult place to reach. In those days it was possible for a student to put together what was needed to buy a bicycle. The problem was the bicycles were often stolen while the students were in class and some of the brightest were affected and unable to continue. Painfully a further twist in the story came to light that the students could have been stealing from each other. Liam Cotter heard of this and scratched his head and then came up with a simple solution. He would build a frame where bicycles could be parked and locked. The idea was accepted and the next day he set to work with his usual thoroughness. The problem was solved there and then. I wonder how many students, now qualified, owe their success to this small act of imagination.

We esteem the famous and the professional. We may feel a sense of awe in the presence of someone who is an expert in his or her chosen field. But better still the leader who is a person of compassion.

7 March, 2009

123

ARCHBISHOP CHICHESTER

Reburials, I suppose, are rare events. The Irish poet W.B. Yeats died in France in 1939 and had to wait until after the second world war before being reburied 'under Ben Bulben' in the west of Ireland. Bishop Shanahan, who trudged the footpaths of eastern Nigeria for twenty years but died in Nairobi in 1943, arrived late for his own second burial in Enugu on a Sunday in 1956. His body made a triumphant spontaneous tour of the surrounding missions for six days before the next Sunday. And now we have our own Aston Ignatius Chichester, first Catholic bishop in then Southern Rhodesia from 1931 to 1956 when he retired. He died as he mounted the steps of St Peter's in Rome at the start of the Second Vatican Council in 1962 and was buried there.

My first reaction to the news that he was being reburied here was a bit like Monica's when she lay dying in Ostia in 387: 'Lay this body wherever it may be,' she told her son Augustine, 'let no care of it disturb you.' This seemed especially relevant when I heard something of the endless red tape and expense of transferring the remains to Harare 47 years after his death. But then I was moved by the actual arrival of the coffin at Chichester Convent in Chishawasha: there was such an outpouring of emotion and awe at what we were witnessing. Some of the old sisters who knew Chichester and who had revered him as the founder of their congregation, the Little Children of Our Blessed Lady, popularly known as LCBL, spoke in deeply affectionate terms directly to him as the coffin lay in their small chapel.

Later the remains were taken to Chishawasha Mission for the burial after a *pungwe* followed by Mass with the present Archbishop, Robert Ndlovu, the fourth after Chichester.

Who was Aston Chichester ('Chic' to his friends) and why all the fuss? He came from an old English family that remained Catholic from Reformation times. He was educated in England and joined the Jesuits there when he was eighteen in 1897. On his appointment as bishop in 1931 he set about building on the foundations already laid by the early missionaries. Besides starting the LCBL Sisters, he established the seminary in Chishawasha for the training of priests. The late Joseph Kubirai wrote of him, 'he was a great leader. He taught you to think.' Lawrence Vambe spoke of him as one who demanded high standards in whatever the students did. At the end of term he would go through the marks and some young student priest would hear the words: 'you did badly in this subject. You must improve, young man.'

There are many stories about him but let two suffice. Before going to bed as a child, his mother taught him to include a Hail Mary for the Pope that he would have a good night. Years later when he was Archbishop and had occasion to meet Pius XI, he ended the conversation by asking him if he had slept well that night. The Pope was surprised but said he had and Chic explained he always said a small prayer that he would.

My other story is of the time he was travelling with another priest and Simon Taoneyi, then boarding master at Chishawasha, and they came to a cluster of branches across a road that served as a gate to stop cattle. The priest saw this impediment and decided to just bulldoze his way through it and drive on. But the bishop stopped him and got out of the car and carefully rebuilt the heap of branches. The priest was no doubt chastened but in a small way it shows the sense of justice and understanding of Chichester. He may not have been in the forefront of the struggle for justice in those days in the 1930s like the Methodist, the Revd

John White, or the Anglican Fr Arthur Shirley Cripps. But all the stories describe a man with a big heart, full of warmth, deep faith, compassion and endless cheerfulness.

14 March 2009

Printed in the United States
By Bookmasters